Albert Palazzo is an adjunct professor at UNSW Canberra in the School of Humanities and Social Sciences. He was formerly the long-serving Director of War Studies for the Australian Army. He completed his PhD in military history at The Ohio State University, and published his dissertation as *Seeking Victory on The Western Front: The British Army and Chemical Warfare in World War I*. Born and raised in Brooklyn, New York, he migrated to Australia in 1996 and commenced his career in the school of history at the Australian Defence Force Academy. He has written more than twenty books and monographs on the art of war, Australian military history and national security policy.

THE BIG FIX

REBUILDING AUSTRALIA'S NATIONAL SECURITY

ALBERT PALAZZO

Melbourne University Publishing acknowledges the traditional owners of the unceded land on which we work, learn and live: the Wurundjeri Woiwurrung peoples of the Kulin Nation. We pay respect to elders past, present and future, and acknowledge the importance of Indigenous knowledge.

MELBOURNE UNIVERSITY PRESS
An imprint of Melbourne University Publishing Limited
Level 1, 715 Swanston Street, Carlton, Victoria 3053, Australia
mup-contact@unimelb.edu.au
www.mup.com.au

First published 2025

Typeset by Sonya Murphy, Adala Studio
Cover design by Design by Committee
Printed in Australia by McPherson's Printing Group

A catalogue record for this book is available from the National Library of Australia

9780522881363 (paperback)
9780522881370 (ebook)

CONTENTS

ABBREVIATIONS

ABF	Australian Border Force
ADF	Australian Defence Force
AI	artificial intelligence
ANZUS	Australia, New Zealand, United States
ASD	Australian Signals Directorate
ASEAN	Association of Southeast Asian Nations
AUKUS	Australia, United Kingdom, United States
CO_2	carbon dioxide
CRS	Congressional Research Service
CSIRO	Commonwealth Scientific and Industrial Research Organisation
CSIS	Center for Strategic & International Studies
DOA	*The Defence of Australia*
DSR	*Defence Strategic Review*
ELSCF	*Enhanced Lethality Surface Combatant Fleet*
GDP	gross domestic product
HIMARS	High Mobility Artillery Rocket System
IIP	*Integrated Investment Program*
LOCSV	Large Optionally Crewed Surface Vessel
NDS	*National Defence Strategy*
OPV	Offshore Patrol Vessels
PLA	People's Liberation Army
ppm	parts per million
PrSM	Precision Strike Missile
RAAF	Royal Australian Air Force
RAN	Royal Australian Navy
SSN	nuclear-powered attack submarine
USAF	United States Air Force
USN	United States Navy
VLS	vertical launch system

INTRODUCTION: BREAKING DEPENDENCY

ON 15 SEPTEMBER 2021, President Joe Biden of the United States joined via a linked video conference the prime ministers of Australia and the United Kingdom, Scott Morrison and Boris Johnson respectively, to announce the formation of a new security relationship to be known as AUKUS, after the initials of the participating countries.[1] The goal of the venture was ostensibly to help sustain the peace and stability of the Indo-Pacific region and to maintain the US-led global rules-based order. The three countries pledged to support each other's security and defence interests, while building on their existing longstanding ties. Prime Minister Morrison had negotiated the agreement in secret and the revelation of its existence took the Australian public, and even most members of Parliament, by surprise. Labor's Shadow Cabinet, and the Leader of the Opposition, Anthony Albanese, received only a twenty-four-hour heads-up.[2]

In creating AUKUS, the security challenge Australia and its partners sought to counter was an increasingly assertive China, under its President, Xi Jinping, and its rapidly improving military. That China is challenging the dominance of the United States in the Western Pacific is well known and the subject of much analysis by military and security commentators.[3] The US military has identified China as its 'pacing threat', by which it means the country against which its forces are to prepare to fight. In addition, the United States is seeking to shore up its alliance system and incorporate its partners into an integrated deterrence network.[4] There is no shortage of flashpoints that could spark a conflict between the great powers, the most concerning being the future of Taiwan and the potential for the renewal of hostilities on the Korean Peninsula.[5]

The Australian government issued its own public statement on the establishment of AUKUS.[6] Morrison explained that Australia needed AUKUS because of the worsening security environment in the Indo-Pacific. Albanese did not hesitate to profess his own support for AUKUS, as well as agreeing on the utility of the deeper relationship with the United States and the United Kingdom that the new arrangement implied. Thus, the leaders of Australia's two main political parties saw eye to eye on the partnership's necessity.[7] Domestic politics was undoubtedly a factor in the government's decision to pursue AUKUS. Albanese, with an eye on the next election, rightly saw the pact as a potential political threat and would not give Morrison a national security issue with which to wedge Labor.[8]

In addition to deepening defence ties, the agreement contained offers of research assistance, access for Australia to hitherto off-limits American weapon systems and a tri-power commitment to greater information and technology sharing. The development of hypersonic missiles, for example, was specifically covered by the agreement. Most significantly of all, the AUKUS partners professed their support for acquiring and operating nuclear-powered submarines by the Australian Defence Force (ADF). Australia would become only the second country to which the United States had granted access to its nuclear submarine secrets, the first being the United Kingdom.[9] Another result of AUKUS was the further integration of the ADF into the US military, including additional opportunities for joint training, port visits and personnel exchanges. The pact should be viewed as a culmination of a trend that sees the two militaries looking for opportunities to work together. Critically, AUKUS served as a revalidation of Australia's position within the American security umbrella. For the United Kingdom, which is no longer a Pacific power, AUKUS provided significantly less, mainly a fleeting opportunity to draw attention to its 'special relationship' with the United States and a sense of nostalgia for an empire past.

On the surface, AUKUS seems like a great deal for Australia, and this is certainly the way Morrison and Albanese have portrayed the agreement. Yet the surface's appealing gloss has diverted attention from AUKUS's many imperfections and inconsistencies, and the leaders of both parties have displayed a lack of critical judgement and national loyalty in their rush to profess their allegiance and their enthusiasm. AUKUS harkens to a time when US power was unchallenged, and constitutes an effort to turn back the tide of history rather than understand it or confront its present realities. In a world facing an existential crisis from climate change, AUKUS epitomises a pact more suited to the Cold War than to the contemporary threat environment. It is neither a courageous defence policy nor a bold exploration of new possibilities. Instead, Morrison and Albanese have perambulated along the well-trodden path of Australia's unbroken reliance on a great power friend for the provision of what, for most states, is a government's ultimate and most important purpose – the security of its territory and people. The agreement also neglects to make a realistic estimate of the probable costs involved, both in Australia's purchase of very expensive platforms and weapon systems, and in the loss of a significant degree of sovereignty and national independence. Australia's leaders have once again positioned the nation so that participation in the United States' next war will be virtually mandatory, even if this is a war between two nuclear-armed great powers. Lastly and most significantly, Australian leaders have assumed the potential menace of China without a commensurate effort to assess either the likelihood of the threat being realised, the potential to mitigate the China challenge without recourse to war or the possibility that there are other risks that are worse. In fact, it would not be too bold to say that AUKUS has made Australia less safe instead of more so.

A further complication is that Australia's expectations of AUKUS may not be matched by the same degree of commitment to which the United States holds the pact. As will be explained in chapter 1, the United States has taken great pains to give itself 'outs' of its own choosing and timing. The return of Donald Trump to the presidency, with his erratic and capricious approach to foreign affairs, also raises concerns for a continued stable relationship between Australia and the United States or for a peaceful resolution to any dispute between the United States and China.

AUKUS is simply the latest manifestation of Australia's routine determination to secure its protection by embracing dependency on a great power. By dependency, I mean the propensity of Australia to seek support from a great power to secure its safety in a world in which it sees threats to the nation's welfare. It was neither an innovative security policy in 1942 when Prime Minister John Curtin announced that Australia would turn to the United States after the failure of the Singapore strategy, nor in 1966 when Prime Minister Harold Holt expressed the nation's enthusiasm to go 'All the way with LBJ' by supporting the United States in the Vietnam War. Australia has never displayed any hesitation in leaning on or clinging to a great power protector, and has proven consistently willing to pay the price, often expressed as the premium on the insurance policy. In embracing dependency, the nation's leaders also dismiss its potential to compromise Australian sovereignty or that it reduces the country to an imperial outpost of its increasingly unstable great power protector.

In its rush to secure the pact, the government has also neglected to explain its necessity to the public. Former diplomat and foreign policy expert Allan Gyngell admitted that he would *like* to be persuaded about the AUKUS project, yet no persuasion has been attempted by the government, not in the form of a speech to Parliament or in any other way.[10] As another commentator noted, 'AUKUS demands more transparency'.[11] What the Australian public has received instead is Morrison's and Albanese's reconfirmation of Australia's place as a junior member of the US Empire, as it was once a junior member of the British Empire, without any further illumination.[12] The two prime ministers have acted on the automatic default setting that has dominated Australia's security decision-making since Federation in 1901, if not before – that is, to seek security by serving as a loyal sub-imperial dependency in a great power's empire. The craving to secure the protection of a great and powerful friend is seemingly hardwired in the psyche of Australia's political leaders.[13] Time will tell if Albanese will be America's next 'deputy sheriff' – an honorific first suggested by the journalist Fred Brenchley during his interview of Prime Minister John Howard for *The Bulletin* in 1999, a term US President George W Bush took up in 2003 – but he is certainly moving in that direction.[14]

The objective of this book is to outline and promote a different and better path for the attainment of Australia's national defence and security, one in which a policy of dependency on a foreign state is not the central feature. It will maintain, despite tradition, that there is no need for Australia to seek security by being reliant on the willingness of a friendly great power to protect it. Nor is there need for Australia to embrace a subservient position to another country, instead of standing on its own. The book will insist that by differentiating between Australian interests and those of its great power protector, it will be possible for us to forge a defence policy that puts Australian security first and does so with a lower degree of risk and cost than is presently the case.

This is not the first effort to promote a non-dependency-based model for Australia. In 1854, John Dunmore Lang, a prominent

Presbyterian clergyman, argued that the colony of New South Wales had nothing to do with Britain's war in the Crimea against Russia and that the Australian colonies should not get involved in Europe's wars. Several years later he returned to this theme by reiterating George Washington's injunction against joining in European alliances because of the danger that it would mandate participation in overseas wars. Such early individuals were able to discriminate between the interests of the Australian colonies and those of Britain – they were not the same, and as the Australian colonies grew and matured as polities their interests would only diverge further. The decision by New South Wales in 1885 to send troops to the Sudan to support the British campaign against the Mahdi was similarly opposed by a vocal minority, but to no avail, and while the contingent was insignificant in number – just 700 men – and arrived after the fighting ended, it set a precedent.[15]

Post Federation, select scholars and military officers have continued to periodically highlight the possibility of other ways to protect Australia from threat.[16] The first occurred in 1913 when two naval officers, Captain Constantine Hughes-Onslow and Commander Hugh Thring, proposed a joint maritime–land defence plan that did not rely on Britian for Australia's security.[17] Others followed at irregular intervals, such as David Martin's *Armed Neutrality for Australia* in 1984.[18] In every case such arguments go unheeded by the government of the day. By contrast, the policy of great power dependency has shown remarkable tenacity and has remained intact for more than 120 years, and today it remains as deeply rooted as ever. I am therefore well aware that the government's aversion to considering other options for safeguarding Australia's national security does not bode well for the success of my own efforts.

However, the timing of this work may prove fortuitous. The government admitted in 2023 that the nation's 'strategic circumstances and the risks we face are now radically different'.[19] Additionally, it is also becoming increasingly clear that the United States is a troubled nation that has lost its confidence and moral authority and is now led by a president who seems intent on challenging existing norms and relationships. Its willingness, or even ability, to act as Australia's protector may be on the wane. It is a well-understood truism that when factors change, policy should also change, or at the very least those in charge should be open to exploring other possibilities. The time, therefore, is ripe for another way.

***

Australia's future security policy is best based on the military philosophy of war known as the Strategic Defensive, rather than a continuation of the present policy of dependency. This is the first time an author has outlined the Strategic Defensive as the optimal military philosophy for Australia while combining it with a critique of the existing ADF force structure and including a description of what the nation actually needs for its security. It is also a rare work in that it recognises climate change as the national security risk it is, instead of limiting itself to traditional state-based threats.

Yet it needs to be recognised that the Strategic Defensive means neither the adoption of neutrality, the embrace of utopian disarmament, nor a retreat into isolationism. Australia would continue to maintain the ADF and fund a well-resourced and powerful military, with the goal of being able to defend its territory and its interests on its own. The ANZUS Alliance could also remain in effect, although it would no longer serve as the foundation of Australian defence, as is presently the case. This change in policy direction would not prevent Australia from going to war as part of a coalition with other states against a common enemy, if the government so decided. What it does mean is that designing, equipping and training the ADF for interoperability with a great power partner would no longer be the force's guiding ambition, as it is now. It also means that Australia would look to itself for its security and, in doing so, become a fully sovereign and independent nation.

To tackle the shortcomings of the present defence policy, and to illuminate the path to a future based on the Strategic Defensive, the book divides into five chapters. Chapter 1 describes Australia's traditional defence policy before diving into the details of the AUKUS agreement, the most consequential defence agreement Australia has entered into since the signing of the ANZUS Treaty in 1951. It will highlight the pact's consequences for the nation, including the signal it sends to the region as Australia recommits to the Anglosphere. Chapter 2 examines the existing threat environment, for which AUKUS is claimed to be the central part of the solution. This chapter will argue that AUKUS's singular focus on China as the threat against which to prepare is a mistake because it ignores the security challenge of a more existential threat, namely climate change. Chapter 3 changes direction to describe the origins and principles of the military philosophy of the Strategic Defensive and shows how its adoption is in the nation's best interests. Chapter 4 addresses the preliminary steps Australia needs to take in order to embrace the Strategic Defensive. Chapter 5 examines the government's present plans for the development of the ADF. It unpacks and evaluates the major capability plans for each of the armed services and explains why most of what the government is acquiring is not in the nation's best interest. In doing so, the chapter will outline what capabilities an ADF organised on Strategic Defensive principles needs. Lastly, the chapter will draw attention to the place of nuclear weapons in the defence of Australia and drill down into the future of the American alliance.

I began to explore the topic during my time as the Director of War Studies in the Australian Army Research Centre, the Army's future-focused 'think-tank'. During my tenure, I wrote a preliminary internal study on the utility of the Strategic Defensive as Australia's future defence policy. Upon leaving the public service, my first task was to write the book *Climate Change and National Security: Implications for the Military*, which the US Army saw value in publishing.[20] I then began to reflect more deeply on the concerns I had over the future relevance of the ADF and the government's predictable and banal responses to what it justifiably saw as a worsening threat environment. The more I considered the situation, the more it became clear that what was needed was a major reconception of the nation's defence requirement, and the resources needed, if genuine security for the Australian people was to result.

I am a long-time member of the Australian security community and have written many books and articles on the nature of war, the nation's future defence and the security challenge of climate change. All too often, in my view, my peers have advocated approaches that simply align with the government's direction. The result has been a tendency towards a uniformity of thought and a reluctance to explore other options. My hope is that this work will motivate the security community to embrace disruptive and divergent thinking, because this is what Australia's political and military leaders need if they are to implement policies that will actually make the nation more secure. In an era marked by increasing insecurity, effective defence requires more than default thinking and a reverence for the preservation of the status quo.

This is my fourteenth book on military history and national security, and one of the things I learned some time ago is that despite my best efforts every work will contain faults. As the author, they are mine and mine alone. I have also learned that none of these works was solely the result of my own analysis, thinking and writing. There are numerous people to whom I owe a debt of gratitude. I would like to especially thank Professor Craig Stockings for the welcome he provided for me in the School of Humanities and Social Sciences at the University of New South Wales – Canberra.

I am also indebted to my mentors at The Ohio State University, Professors Allan R Millett and the late Williamson Murray, who instilled in me the skills that have underpinned all my work. They put me on the path that has led to this book. It is from my father, Albert E Palazzo, that I inherited my love for military history. He could never have foreseen the effect all those battlefield visits in my childhood would have had on a young mind, for which I am grateful. I would like to recognise my children Albert, Thomas, Margaret and William to whom the future belongs and to whom *The Big Fix* is dedicated. Lastly, it is to my extraordinary wife, Melissa Benyon, to whom I owe the greatest debt and thanks.

1

UNDERSTANDING AUKUS

WHAT DOES AUKUS MEAN for Australia's defence policy and for the security of Australia and its people? AUKUS is the most recent defence initiative undertaken by the Australian government and, if it stands, will shape Australia's security policy well into the future. Its place in the nation's security is much more than just continuity with Australia's longstanding tradition of dependency on a great power partner for security. It is also much more than simply an intensification of an existing relationship with old friends. Rather, as Andrew Fowler explains in his book *Nuked*, it represents an unprecedented surrender of sovereignty as Australia's leaders tie the nation's future to that of the United States, while revealing to their voters as little information as possible to justify the most expensive defence commitment in the country's history.[1]

The establishment of AUKUS is important, not only for what the leaders of its partner countries have said but also for what they have implied. It is necessary, therefore, to understand the nuances that underpin the willingness of the United States, the United

Kingdom and Australia to work together to mitigate the security concerns they have over the future of their position in the Western Pacific and Indian oceans. Any agreement between states comes with obligations, and this chapter strives to throw light on what AUKUS will demand of Australia.

The government has placed little information on AUKUS on the public record: the full scope of AUKUS – its benefits and the obligations it contains and will generate, as well as much of the financial implications for the taxpayer – remains opaque and shrouded in secrecy. The text of the agreement has not been provided to the public, nor have the discussion documents or meeting minutes created during its two-year negotiation period. The best the Australian people have received is a 2022 fact sheet summarising the pact's achievements to date.[2] However, despite this lack of information it is clear that AUKUS fits well within the Australian security tradition.

The Australian tradition of national security

Australia's leaders have maintained a defence policy of dependency on a great power protector with consistency, uniformity, loyalty, and absence of imagination throughout the nation's history.[3] There have been modifications, but only at the margins or in the rhetoric, and these did not materially change the substance of the practice. Australia's defence policy has proven so durable that it has easily survived changes in leaders, governing parties and security partners, as well as global upheavals. Originally, the great power protector was the United Kingdom and since the Second World War it has been the United States.

The means by which Britain provided for Australia's security was through the ships of the Royal Navy. A 1901 report prepared in London by the Colonial Defence Committee explained the importance of the imperial fleet to the well-being of Australia:

> The maintenance of British supremacy at sea is the first condition of the security of Australian territory and trade in war. Such supremacy implies that no organized attack will be directed against any port of Australia and that the maritime communication between Australian ports and the rest of the world will be kept free from sustained interruption.[4]

Essentially, the imperial fleet would safeguard the new nation's territory as well as its most vital interest: the Commonwealth's trade with other parts of the empire and the world.[5] While the Royal Navy served as the ultimate security guarantor, this did not mean that Australia could do without a military of its own. It still needed a small land force to provide for internal protection, defence against raids, and the staffing of the coastal defences that guarded the harbours the fleet would need.[6]

Having allocated responsibility for the continent's defence to Britain, Australia's new government did not hesitate to cede another government lever of power – foreign affairs. At a meeting in the Melbourne Town Hall, Australia's first Prime Minister, Edmund Barton, declared, as reported by *The Sydney Morning Herald*, that 'There could be no foreign policy of the Commonwealth. The foreign policy belonged to the Empire'.[7] The statement was apparently met with cheers and required no explanation to those in attendance. They shared Barton's understanding that they were members of a vast empire and accepted the need for it to speak with a single voice – a voice that emanated from London. Barton noted that in matters concerning the Pacific that were of importance to Australia, firm yet courteous representation would be made to London, but in most instances, Britain would represent Australia to the world.[8]

When the First World War broke out there was never any doubt that Australians would fight alongside their British cousins, along with the members of the other dominions. Imperial loyalty resonated with most of the Australian population, and it proved no difficulty to balance commitment to the Empire with an emerging sense of nationhood. As historian Joan Beaumont observes, the language of empire dominated the memorials built to commemorate the war's dead, the four causes most commonly cited being God, king, empire and country.[9] The word 'Australia' rarely appears. For those designing the memorials, 'Australia is both synonym for country and subsumed under empire'.[10]

After the First World War, Australia and the United Kingdom codified their traditional but informal defence relationship with a policy known as the Singapore Strategy. Presented at the 1923 Committee of Imperial Defence, the plan called for the British fleet to sail from its home waters to its base at Singapore, from which it would undertake operations against enemy warships threatening Australia, New Zealand or other parts of the Empire. Australia always assumed the enemy would be Japan. The policy created a comforting illusion of security for seventeen years, but it was not without vocal opposition. Army officers, for example, pointed out with prescience that the Japanese would choose to strike when Britain was fully engaged elsewhere, such as in the event of a war in Europe.[11] Following the surrender of France to Germany and Italy on 17 June 1940, fears intensified in Canberra that Japan would take advantage of Britain's distraction and attack. Two days later, Australia received word from London that the fleet would not sail to its aid – the Royal Navy's priority was to secure the British Isles.[12]

As tensions with Japan reached the point of no return, and with Britain fully engaged in a desperate struggle with Germany and Italy, Australia's great power protector managed to spare just two major warships, the *Prince of Wales* and *Repulse,* for the Far East. Shortly after the commencement of the Pacific War, Japanese aircraft sank both when they sortied from Singapore. On 15 February 1942, Singapore capitulated to the Japanese, and more than 130 000 imperial troops went into captivity, including most of the

Australian 8th Division. The failure of the Singapore Strategy signalled the urgent need for Australia to find a new protector. Already at war with Germany, Britain did not have the strength to defeat Japan as well. Nothing further of substance could be forthcoming from the imperial fleet, a reality that led Australian Prime Minister John Curtin to announce on 27 December 1941 that 'Without any inhibitions of any kind, I make it quite clear that Australia looks to America, free of any pangs as to our traditional links or kin-ship with the United Kingdom'.

In doing so Curtin accepted the reality that Britain's first obligation was to the British people. Australia was at the periphery of an empire, an outlying province that needed the centre more than the centre needed it. It was time to switch protectors. Curtin recognised that in the eyes of Britain it would be acceptable:

> [t]hat Australia can go, and Britain can still hold on. We are therefore determined that Australia shall not go, and we shall exert all our energies toward the shaping of a plan, with the United States as its keystone, which will give to our country some confidence of being able to hold out until the tide of battle swings against the enemy.[13]

Curtin was not expressing a new sentiment – Australia had been making overtures to the United States for some time, but had consistently been rebuffed. In mid-1939, Curtin's predecessor as Prime Minister, Robert Menzies, felt it necessary to warn Cabinet there was no certainty that the United States would aid the British Empire if the Japanese attacked. It was to give Australia a stronger voice in Washington that Menzies authorised the establishment of an embassy, the nation's first. Richard Casey took up the post in February 1940 and soon discovered that there was not a lot of interest in Australia. While Australia was a friend, it was not a friend of such importance as to warrant a security commitment.[14]

It was very late in the crisis when the United States began to show an interest in Australia. What led to the American change in attitude was a desire by the US military to establish an alternative reinforcement and sustainment route to the Philippines, one that did not traverse Japan's central Pacific territories. In mid-October 1940, the United States formally approached Australia for basing rights at airfields across the north of the country and in New Guinea. The Americans wanted access to Rabaul, Port Moresby, Townsville and Darwin, which US aircraft would use on their journey to Manila. A few days later, the request expanded to include the right to conduct training and familiarisation flights from these bases as well as to construct maintenance depots, fuel and bomb storage areas and communication facilities. The United States next requested permission to extend the runway at Townsville so that it could service its B-17 four-engine bombers. Additional access requests followed when the Americans sought to add Cloncurry and Daly Waters to the list of allowed airfields, as well as to build dispersal fields and a repair facility in Brisbane. Sensing an opportunity to attract American military support to Australia, the Curtin government approved all these requests.[15] In a reprise of 1940 amid growing tensions with China, Australia agreed in 2022 to the positioning of US Air Force B-52 bombers at RAAF Base Tindal, while in October 2024 US B-2 Spirit bombers launched on attack on Yemen from RAAF Base Amberley.[16] In Darwin, the Pentagon also constructed 300 million litres of jet fuel storage for use by its aircraft. As befitting an imperial power, the United States built the fuel tanks without the permission of the Northern Territory Government, although one assumes the requisite permits will be forthcoming.

Australians should realise that the purpose of these planes, improved runways and fuel storage tanks is not to protect Australia. America's interest in Darwin and Brisbane is that it allows it to move valuable aircraft from Guam and Okinawa to locations more remote from Chinese attack while still being able to conduct operations. Of course, in demonstrating its loyalty as an ally, the Australian government has accepted the consequence of making the country more of a target if hostilities were to eventuate between the United States and China.[17] Nor is this the first time the B-52 will have operated out of Darwin. Since the 1980s these planes have been regular visitors, conducting surveillance operations over the Indian Ocean or training runs across Australia.

In early 1942, Australia did not rate as a priority in the eyes of US leaders, and it never would. General Dwight D Eisenhower, then serving as Chief of the War Plans Division in Washington, ranked Australia's security at sixth on a list of eight 'things that are highly desirable'. Australia did not even make it onto his list of things that were necessary for the defeat of the Axis powers.[18] Unsurprisingly, Australia saw the war through the limited vision of a small power distantly located from friends, and consequently prioritised its own needs. By contrast, the United States as a great power conceived the war on a global scale and planned in terms of what it needed to do to achieve victory. Such distinct points of view are fundamental to coalitions and this particular difference in perspective remains in place to this day.

After the Second World War ended, Australia's courtship of the United States intensified. Australia and New Zealand wanted a formal security agreement with the United States. Despite the three countries having recently been comrades in arms, the United States was decidedly unenthusiastic about a pact linking them, and consistently refused the suggestion. The US Secretary of State, Dean Acheson, explained that because of geography Australia was not a priority for the United States. For the United States, Japan and North Asia were important, the South-West Pacific was, unfortunately for Australia, not. If Australia wanted to be secure, Acheson suggested, it would need to rely first on its own resources and then upon the collective security provided by the United Nations.[19]

When Australia's Minister for External Affairs, Percy Spender, visited the United States in mid-1950 he had high hopes for the negotiation of a security treaty. To his surprise the Americans were not interested and the talks, while friendly, went nowhere.[20] It was the Korean War and the threat of communist expansion that gave Australia and New Zealand the leverage they required to push the United States to agree to a mutual defence treaty. In order to create a bulwark against communist expansion in North-East Asia, the United States believed a rearmed and democratic Japan was a necessity. Therefore, the United States wanted to grant Japan a soft peace treaty, one that Australia and New Zealand would also agree to. However, both countries distrusted a rearmed Japan and expressed their displeasure over the absence of a tri-nation security agreement with which to ease their anxiety. To convince Australia and New Zealand to accept the soft peace treaty, the United States gave way and met the demands of its junior partners. The result was the ANZUS Treaty, a quid pro quo agreement in which the level of interest of the member parties was unequal from the start. For Australia and New Zealand, ANZUS was the essential cornerstone of future security, while for the United States it was a reluctant commitment given graciously but without any deep significance.[21]

With the signing of ANZUS, the Australian government saw the United States as its protector; a perception that continues to reverberate through defence policy documents to the present. For example, while the *2016 Defence White Paper* identifies Australia's first strategic objectives as 'to deter, deny and defeat any attempt by a hostile state or non-state actor to attack, threaten or coerce Australia', it admits that this objective nests within the context of the ANZUS Alliance. The White Paper describes ANZUS as 'a strong and deep alliance at the core of Australia's security and defence planning', and recognises that 'Australia's security is underpinned by the ANZUS Treaty'.[22]

Moreover, the United States also safeguards Australia's broader interests. The *2016 Defence White Paper* summarises this as follows: 'The presence of the United States military forces plays a vital role in ensuring security across the Indo-Pacific and the global strategic and economic weight of the United States will be essential to the continued effective functioning of the rules-based global order'.[23]

Even *The Defence of Australia (DOA)* white paper (1987), whose intent was to advance Australian self-reliance, maintained the need for an ongoing dependency on the United States for protection. *DOA* states that the government's acceptance of self-reliance is the minimum standard to be expected of any self-respecting country and goes on to say that 'Australia can scarcely pretend to contribute to the defence of broader Western interests if it cannot defend itself'.[24] The paper then identifies the various benefits the ANZUS Treaty provides to Australia, including the deterrence effect of port visits by US warships, training enhancements through participation in combined exercises and access to the US intelligence system and advanced technologies. Lastly, the report claims that the 'defence relationship with the United States gives confidence that in the event of a fundamental threat to Australia's security, US military support would be forthcoming'.[25]

Australia's most recent defence policy document, the 2023 *National Defence: Defence Strategic Review* (*DSR*), concurs with previous defence reviews and states that 'Australia's strategic culture has long been based on a major power alliance. Every Australian Government since Federation has assessed our strategic circumstances and reaffirmed the centrality of an alliance partnership in relationship to our strategic interests'. The document goes on to affirm that for the future it anticipates 'our Alliance with the United States ... becoming even more important to Australia'.[26]

Australian politicians take every opportunity to reiterate the importance of the United States to Australia's security. Speaking in Washington, after just two months in government, the Minister for Defence, Richard Marles, declared that 'the US–Australian alliance has become a cornerstone of Australia's foreign policy'.[27] In announcing his upcoming visit to Washington in Parliament, Albanese made sure to dwell on the deep history and shared vision between the two countries and to restate that the alliance was the main pillar of Australia's foreign policy.[28]

To close the gap between the Australian government's threat perception and its unwillingness to provide the requisite defence capability from the country's own resources, it has maintained a defence policy of remarkable resilience and continuity. While the cost of offshoring national defence has been the periodic need to participate in a war as a junior partner, the nation's leaders consistently saw this as a small price to pay for the sense of security Britain and the United States offered, as well as an opportunity to lower defence costs and redirect the savings to other needs.

The price of dependency

To most observers, Australia's policy of dependency has been a success. Australia remains a free and independent country, it has never been conquered and its people enjoy an enviable lifestyle. The Japanese did attack Darwin and other places during the Second World War, but they had no intention to occupy the continent. Moreover, once the United States deployed its strength, it progressively pushed the Japanese back until the enemy's home islands were within sight. For the future, as the government acknowledges in the 2023 *DSR*, there remains little chance of any adversary attempting to invade Australia.[29]

Australia has maintained its membership in two successive empires for reasons that go beyond a fear of invasion. The historian Clinton Fernandes has best expressed the true goal of Australia's security policy: Australia actively wants to be a sub-imperial power within a great power's empire.[30] The status of a sub-imperial power has benefits because it allows Australia to leverage the great partner's latent power for its own purposes. For example, after Federation, as parliamentarians came together to provide the new nation's laws, the political issue that dominated their time was the establishment of the White Australia Policy. The parliamentary debates on the matter show a membership that had no hesitancy to treat most of the world's inhabitants as lesser peoples. Australia needed the Royal Navy, not so much to protect Australian territory from invasion, but to make sure that no Asian nation could bring pressure onto Australia to allow non-European migrants into the country, resulting in what parliamentarians feared would be the 'adulteration' of the 'white race'. During the Versailles Peace Conference following the conclusion of the First World War, the Australian Prime Minister, Billy Hughes, fought hard against the inclusion in the League of Nations' covenant a clause establishing the principle of racial equality. Its proposal was the work of the Japanese delegation. Hughes believed the Japanese would use even the most minor affirmation of racial equality as a wedge to pry open Australia's borders. For Hughes, Australia had not sacrificed so much in the war to lose the battle for a white Australia in the peace. With British, dominion and American support, Hughes prevailed.[31]

After the Second World War, Australia turned to the US Empire and its spirit of international corporatism and consumer materialism. Australia has been a ready participant in the post-war global rules-based order that the United States has established and sustained, and has consistently voiced support for it. The language in the 2023 *DSR* is unambiguous: 'The defence of Australia's national interests lies in the protection of our economic connection with the world and the maintenance of the global rules-based order'. The present threat to the global rules-based order, the report did not hesitate to identify, was China.[32] To Australia's leaders it must seem supremely ironic that under the Trump presidency the greatest threat to the global rules-based order could now turn out to be the United States.

Allan Gyngell, in his book *Fear of Abandonment*, outlines why the rules-based order is of such importance to Australia:

> The international order established by the winners at the end of World War II had suited Australia perfectly. It was based on liberal values like Australia's own, structured around multilateral institutions and underpinned by the dominant power of the United States. American support for open international trade helped drive unprecedented global growth, while its network of alliances in Europe and Asia provided a stable security framework.[33]

Imperial membership comes with costs, however. The most obvious are the lives lost and the money spent in wars in which Australia chooses to participate, not out of military necessity but out of what historian David Horner has called political considerations. Horner states that from 1944 onwards, the forces Australia has contributed to military operations have had no effect on any outcome.[34] Australia has not been required to commit to these conflicts – from Korea to Iraq – but has done so out of a perceived need to demonstrate its support to the United States. For some conflicts, such as the Vietnam War, Australia basically insisted on its own participation in order to be seen as supporting the American intervention. A post–Vietnam War report, prepared under the direction of Gough Whitlam when he was the prime minister, illustrates the government's policy of working with the United States. It leaves no doubt that Australia's participation in the war was political not military: Australia's policy was to encourage American military commitment to Asia. The government believed that having a US military presence in the region was the best means by which to prevent an expansion of communism in Australia's direction. The Americans did not actually need Australian military assistance – the Australian contribution even at its peak was trivial – but the United States did appreciate the presence of friends which demonstrated to the world that it was not alone in its opposition to communism in South-East Asia.[35]

The consistent driving motivation by the leaders of both main political parties was to avoid giving the United States any cause to abandon Australia.[36] The need to placate the United States exposes one of the greatest dangers that rests dormant within the AUKUS agreement. Kurt Campbell, the US AUKUS negotiator, knows that Australia has strategically chained itself, as has the United Kingdom, to the policies of the United States. Speaking at the Center for Strategic & International Studies (CSIS) he observed: 'The strategic significance of AUKUS is that both Australia and Great Britain have made a fundamental decision to align with us strategically, not just now, but ... into the distant future'.[37]

As one US admiral commented, AUKUS is 'a forever endeavor'.[38] The defence strategist Hugh White has concluded that AUKUS was Biden's means to get Australia off the fence and to lock its allegiance to America for the next forty years.[39] Moreover, Australia has sold itself cheaply and obtained no guarantees, including the delivery of the promised Virginia-class submarines which remains at the discretion of the United States, a fact the 2024 Naval Nuclear Propulsion Treaty makes clear.[40] Perhaps such a 'chain-like bond' would have always been the result, but AUKUS makes any independent Australian defence policy that much harder to achieve.

Australia has decided to contribute troops to US causes even when it had a fundamental difference of opinion on the necessity for the war. For example, in the lead-up to the 2003 Iraq War, the National Security Cabinet met to agree on a policy for the war. The meeting revealed a tension between Australian and US war aims. The US goal was regime change whereas the Australian objective focused on the elimination of weapons of mass destruction.[41]

Australia has dispatched its military willingly and in some cases on operations of dubious legal standing, such as the 2003 US-led invasion of Iraq. The foreign policy priority of John Howard, after he became prime minister in 1996, was to improve Australia's relationship with the United States. This resulted in Australia's participation in the Afghanistan and Iraq wars, both of which the United States would eventually lose and lose badly. Australia's contribution to both conflicts was hardly noticeable in military terms, but for the Americans all that mattered on the international stage was having Australia's flag alongside their own. Not only were both wars a disastrous failure for the United States and a tragedy for the people of Afghanistan and Iraq, they also morally compromised the personnel Australia committed.

Those serving in the ADF know that the objective of all wars is to compel the enemy to do one's will. A state goes to war with a goal in mind and its military strives to force the enemy to accede to it. Politicians who oversee the waging of Australia's wars and who provide the resources the military requires should understand this too. To achieve compulsion, pressure is applied upon the enemy's forces, usually by violence, that wears down the adversary's physical and psychological ability to resist. In Afghanistan, after Australia's 2006 re-engagement in that conflict, and from the start of the Iraq War, the ADF did not seek to do this. In both of these wars, Australian military personnel certainly inflicted death and destruction on the enemy, as well as an unknown number of civilians, but the target of this violence was never the enemy's will to resist. Rather, the object of ADF's warfighting was to influence the perception of Australia's worth and allegiance in the minds of America's political and military leadership. Australia fought these wars to enhance the alliance with the United States, and the eventual outcome in Afghanistan and Iraq was immaterial to this goal. Prime Minister Howard dispatched Australian forces to win the hearts and minds of the American leadership, and in doing so morally compromised these personnel.

To limit war's destructive effect, particularly against noncombatants, states have agreed to a set of rules, which unfortunately are not always followed. One of the critical ones is the concept of proportionality. This means that in the application of force one can only use the amount required for the task and not more. For example, if enemy forces are occupying a building, you can legally and morally destroy that building and kill all inside, but you cannot destroy the entire neighbourhood and kill or wound all who live there. In these wars, since the enemy's will to resist was not the actual target, the violence Australian forces directed against the insurgents in Iraq and the Taliban in Afghanistan from 2006 did not meet the standard of proportionality. Neither how much nor how little force Australians used, nor how the enemy reacted, was instrumental to achieving the government's war goal, because the true war goal was the good will of the Americans and the reinforcement of the alliance with the United States. The only proportionate amount of force that Australia could have legally and morally used in these wars was none.

Dependency comes with baggage that has been consistently ignored by the Australian government in its desire to be seen as supportive of its great power partner, whether the United Kingdom or the United States. This dependency has never been about safeguarding Australian territory from invasion, since the nation has never faced that threat. It has always been about protecting Australian interests. There is nothing wrong with this in principle, but when a state misrepresents its purpose, including to its own citizens, the moral equation changes. Other nations have never had the intent to despoil Australia, nor was our participation in the Vietnam War really about halting the expansion of communism. Australia's goal in these wars was to focus US attention on our part of the world. The failure to openly acknowledge Australia's true purpose in going to war has cost our nation more than lives and money. It has also cost honour.

Unpacking AUKUS

To call the 15 September 2021 announcement of the AUKUS agreement a surprise would be an understatement. In an age of leaks, hacks and social media revelations, the governments of Australia, the United Kingdom and the United States successfully kept a close hold on the fact of the pact's existence through two years of negotiation up until its announcement. If the Australian public was not in the loop, it can draw consolation from the fact that neither was Emmanuel Macron, the President of France. Australia had a contract with the French company Naval Group for the construction of conventionally powered submarines. Obviously, with the prospect of obtaining nuclear-powered submarines, there was no longer a need for the French boats. Morrison cancelled the contract just hours before the announcement of AUKUS, an act that drew strong condemnation from Macron and the recall of the French ambassador from Canberra. The French Foreign Minister, Jean-Yves Le Drian, described the AUKUS announcement as constituting 'unacceptable behaviour among allies and partners'.[42] Nearly a year later it was up to Albanese to thaw Australia's icy relations with France, as well as to agree to pay a €555 million contract break fee.[43] AUKUS also came as a surprise to Australia's most important neighbour – Indonesia. The Indonesian Ministry of Foreign Affairs issued a formal statement of its deep concern over the 'continuing arms race and power projection in the region' while taking cautious note of Australia's decision to acquire nuclear-powered submarines.[44] It is hardly surprising that China voiced its disappointment at AUKUS and Australia's plan to acquire these warships, labelling the initiative a 'dangerous precedent' as well as provocative and destabilising.[45] Not unreasonably, the Chinese view AUKUS as part of an anti-China military clique.

The AUKUS partners divide the initiative into two pathways, or pillars. The focus of Pillar I is on the nuclear-powered submarines (SSNs) and on the related requirements for the RAN to be able to operate, crew, sustain and repair these complex and lethal warships. Pillar I will see the rotational deployment of US and UK SSNs to Western Australia. To speed up Australia's nuclear-powered submarine ambitions the United States is expected to sell Australia three to five Virginia-class SSNs at some point in the 2030s, thereby reducing its own fleet of operational boats. There is also to be a co-designed AUKUS-class SSN that will enter service in the 2040s ... or so. Australia hopes to have eight boats of its own – eventually.[46] The focus of Pillar II is on accelerating the development and delivery of advanced military capabilities through information sharing and research collaboration.

Pillar I is the more visible and glamorous of the two pathways. It is also the better defined and has a clear and measurable endpoint – Australia's ownership and operation of nuclear-powered submarines. Yet despite receiving the bulk of attention from the government, security commentators and the media, Pillar I is the least important of the two pathways. Pillar I's objective is the acquisition of a known capability that carries known weapons, and represents a known warfighting system that China also possesses and knows how to operate. The RAN's Virginia boats are existing ones that will come from the US fleet, and the future AUKUS submarine will not arrive until well into the 2040s. While Australia's acquisition of SSNs enhances the RAN's potency and status among the world's navies, it does nothing to improve the overall future warfighting strength of the three partners until the second half of the century and only if the program is a success.

In comparison with Pillar I's clarity, Pillar II is undeveloped, undefined and lacks a simple and easily expressed endpoint. The technologies that fall under Pillar II are wide-ranging, and the monies required and objectives aimed for are largely unknown. Among the host of areas for investigation are artificial intelligence, uncrewed undersea vehicles, quantum technologies, deep space advanced radars, hypersonic and counter-hypersonic missile systems, and cyber security. To facilitate advances in these technologies the three partners have also agreed to share information. Pillar II is the pathway that has the potential to lead to a breakthrough in weapons or systems that will provide the AUKUS partners with the means to achieve an asymmetric advantage over the Chinese military. Pillar II technologies also have the potential to arrive in Australia much sooner than the AUKUS-designed SSNs, which will not come into service for another two decades or more. In fact, such is the promise of Pillar II that one could question if Pillar I should even exist, other than for political messaging. The AUKUS partners need to scope Pillar II more completely and act with even greater urgency than they have done to date, along with providing the necessary funding.[47]

In addition to looking to the future, AUKUS has facilitated Australia's access to existing weapon systems that the United States rarely makes available to its allies and partners. For example, in August 2023, the Australian government announced the purchase of 200 Tomahawk missiles as part of a deal worth A$1.7 billion. The Tomahawk has been the mainstay of the US military's distant strike capability since its introduction in 1983. Upon delivery, Australia will become only the second country outside of the United States that is allowed to receive it, the other – of course – being the United Kingdom. The Minister for Defence, Richard Marles, has justified the rationale for these missiles as being their ability to hold an adversary as far away from our shores as possible and, thereby, keep Australians safe.[48] Whether or not the Tomahawk is a useful addition to the ADF arsenal will be considered in chapter 5.

Under Pillar I, a number of preliminary requirements are under way to prepare the ADF for the submarines when they eventually arrive. These include increasing education and training opportunities for RAN personnel at US and UK nuclear-focused schools. At the end of 2023, the RAN graduated its first sailors from these institutions. Defence industry workers are also receiving enhanced training and the first tranches of yard workers have already commenced work in the Pearl Harbor Navy Shipyard in Hawaii and the Barrow-in-Furness Shipyard in England. Additionally, RAN sailors commenced duty in Guam in early 2024 to build their nuclear-powered submarine maintenance skills and qualifications in order to service US and UK boats when they visit Australia. In 2024, the first tranche of RAN sailors joined the crews of US Virginia boats.[49]

Another aspect of the AUKUS agreement is the increased number of visits to HMAS *Stirling* in Western Australia by US and UK boats. The USS *North Carolina* docked at *Stirling* in August 2023, and other US boats have followed. The United Kingdom has pledged to have its nuclear submarines visit Australia, beginning in 2026.[50] It is expected that US and UK SSNs will undergo some of their maintenance in Australia – the USS *Hawaii*, for example, underwent a maintenance period at HMAS *Stirling* in September 2024.[51]

On 13 March 2023, Albanese joined Biden and the new British Prime Minister, Rishi Sunak, in San Diego to outline the progress to date, particularly the SSN program. The announcement made four major points:

- Australian military and civilian personnel would embed within US and UK submarines and industrial bases in order to accelerate the training of Australian personnel.
- By 2027, the United States and the United Kingdom would commence forward rotations of nuclear-powered submarines to Australia.
- Starting in the 2030s the United States would sell Australia three used Virginia-class submarines, assuming congressional approval.
- In the early 2040s Australia would deliver its first SSN-AUKUS, a new class of SSN jointly designed by the United Kingdom and Australia.[52]

The AUKUS partners also used the occasion to renew their commitment to a free and open Indo-Pacific and the upholding of the – increasingly shaky – rules-based international order.[53]

In August 2024, the three partners announced the latest advance in the AUKUS program. They signed a treaty on the transfer of nuclear propulsion materials from the United States and the United Kingdom to Australia.[54]

The consequences of AUKUS

Despite the hype from Morrison and Albanese, the details of the AUKUS agreement remain largely a mystery. Until the confidential terms of the agreement are publicly available, no one can know or assess with any precision the obligations Australia has incurred, or whether the touted benefits will eventuate as promised. It is likely, however, that the obligations will be similar to those Australia has accepted in the past, namely to support the United States in its international objectives and receive in return the 'pinky promise' of a great power's protection. Sustaining and maintaining the US relationship has been the mainstay of Australian national security policy, and signalling fealty to its protector continues to be a responsibility willingly embraced by Australia's political leaders. Such is Australia's relationship with the United States that it has become, as one scholar describes it, 'a political institution in its own right, comparable with a political party or the monarchy'.[55] Political scientist Coral Bell, in her book *Dependent Ally*, labels Australia's dependency on the United States 'a persistent national addiction'.[56]

AUKUS is simply a continuation of the policy of exchanging dependency for the promise of security. That the security environment of the Western Pacific is changing rapidly is a known event. However, by continuing to defer to past policy, with the only change being a greater degree of integration, Australia has again declined the opportunity to undertake a bolder and more visionary threat and risk assessment of its security requirements. Dependency has also necessitated minimising other threats, such as climate change. The effect of AUKUS on Australia's ability to conduct an independent threat and risk assessment will be explored more deeply in chapter 2.

AUKUS will also necessitate an increase in defence spending. At present, no one can say how much more money will be needed because most of the AUKUS-generated programs have not been fully costed, or in many cases even defined. Nuclear-powered submarines do not come cheap, even used ones, and the ADF will not be able to repurpose sufficient funds indefinitely from other parts of the defence budget. At some point, real additional money will be required if Australia is to obtain and operate the subs, whose estimated cost, as of March 2023, was A$368 billion. The SSN purchase is Australia's single most expensive defence acquisition in over 120 years of nationhood. The Pillar II pathway will also require significant funding as the AUKUS partners aim to investigate, develop, acquire and operate a host of new technologies.[57]

Some may be tempted to decry the SSN project's cost in terms of how the money could be better used for other government services such as hospitals or schools. However, this book is about Australian security and I do not share the belief that the defence budget is already too robust. In fact, my belief is the opposite. In an age of increasing international threats more money will need to be spent on defence if Australia is to remain secure. How and where the government allocates this money is the question, and it is from this perspective that the SSN and other defence projects fall short. The opportunity cost is that Australia will not acquire weapon systems that would offer greater utility and a better prospect of protecting the continent than a fleet of around eight submarines will do twenty years from now – as explained in chapter 5.

Perhaps the greatest consequence of agreeing to AUKUS is that Australia has made itself hostage to US policy. On 15 December 2023, the Australian Department of Defence issued a media release on the passage of the 2024 *National Defense Authorization Act* by the US Congress. This was an important event, because among its many US-centric sections and clauses was authorisation to sell three Virginia-class SSNs to Australia, as well as other provisions that would facilitate the development of the nuclear submarine program. Marles described the passage as a 'historic reform that will transform our ability to effectively deter, innovate and operate together'. The media release described the US legislation as a 'game-changer for Australia, the United Kingdom and the United States' and claimed that it would 'enhance our individual and collective capacity to support security, peace and prosperity in the Indo-Pacific'.[58]

What the 15 December media release did not say was that US agreement to the SSN transfer was conditional on what might be termed Australia's good behaviour. In particular, the 2024 *National Defense Authorization Act* imposed two sets of three conditions each on the transfer of the submarines to Australia. They are that the transfer:

1 will not degrade the United States undersea capabilities;
2 is consistent with United States foreign policy and national security interests; and
3 is in furtherance of the AUKUS partnership.

And that:

4 the United States is making sufficient submarine production and maintenance investments to meet the combinations of United States military requirement and the requirement under points 1 to 3;
5 the government of Australia has provided the appropriate funds and support for the additional capacity required to meet the requirements identified in this section; and
6 the Government of Australia has the capability to host and fully operate the vessels authorized to be transferred.

Unfortunately, achieving some of the terms are not within Australia's remit – success depends solely on the degree of success the United States has in meeting its own requirements. In addition, for the transfer of a vessel or vessels to occur, the US president must certify to Congress, with not less than 270 days' notice, that the conditions outlined above (points 1 to 6) have been met.[59]

The 2024 Naval Nuclear Propulsion Treaty codifies the right of the United States to change its mind about the submarine transfer. Article One allows the United States to keep its submarines if it believes their sale would 'constitute an unreasonable risk to its defence and security'. In addition, scattered throughout the treaty are other opportunities for the United States to cancel the transfer, such as if Australia fails to build a storage facility for the submarines' nuclear waste. Nowhere in the treaty is there any penalties for the United States if it fails to follow through on the transfer, nor any suggestion of compensation to Australia for the billions of dollars it would have wasted.[60]

In an echo of Barton's Melbourne Town Hall speech, Australia has in effect accepted a quid-pro-quo requirement for the SSN acquisition. It took from Federation until 1942 for Australia to become independent in foreign affairs. In 2024, Australia took a step backwards. While the terms of the 2024 *National Defense Authorization Act* that relate to Australia are a minuscule part of what is a vast law, they are important for Australia because they impose behaviour constraints for which there could be consequences – no subs – if Australia transgresses. Amazingly, the Act includes no limitation on the worldwide US interests that Australia must support even if they are contrary to Australian interests. Australian loyalty to the United States is such that the limits on independence contained in the transfer conditions were probably unnecessary, but Barton understood more than 120 years ago that Australia was a separate country, if a subset of an empire. The passage of time has seen little progress in Australia's perception of its own status.

The conditions listed above mean that the United States has scope to cancel the SSN deal on technical, financial, operational or – perhaps most alarmingly – domestic political grounds. Further exposing Australia is the fact that the US president's necessary certification is a subjective one. Since the AUKUS agreement was the work of the Biden administration it was unlikely that he would have sunk the deal. President Trump is not bound by similar sentiment and could cancel the agreement without cause and without recourse for Australia. Since the delivery of the SSNs will not occur until well into the future, Australia must run the risk of several presidents, with different world views and personalities, who might see little benefit in the AUKUS arrangement. Australia would be wise to recognise this very real risk as it expends time, effort and money to meet the requirements for the SSN transfer.

Of additional concern is the fact that the United States already has numerous reasons for cancelling the SSN transfer. A report prepared for Congress by the Congressional Research Service (CRS) highlighted the deal's pros and cons. The CRS prepared the report in order to provide Congress with sufficient information to decide whether or not to include the SSN transfer in the 2024 *National Defense Authorization Act*.

In passing the Act, Congress clearly saw an overall benefit in allowing the SSN transfer to move ahead. This was despite a number of potential negative outcomes on US combat capability that the CRS brought to Congress's attention. These included:

- the effect the sale of three Virginia-class SSNs would have on the number and availability of US boats;
- the possible weakening of the SSN deterrence effect if China believed the RAN would operate its boats less effectively than the United States Navy (USN);
- the recognition that Australia could decide not to participate in a US–China conflict over Taiwan or to use its SSNs in a manner incompatible with US preferences; and
- a lessening of overall deterrence capability because of a reduction

in other Australian military capabilities due to pressure on the defence budget as a result of the SSN acquisition.

The effects of the last point are already being seen. The Department of Defence has cancelled or cut back a number of projects in order to shift money to the SSN acquisition.

The report also pointed out that the most cost-effective and militarily efficient approach to the SSN question would be to pursue a US–Australia division of labour. This would see US SSNs perform both American and Australian SSN missions, encouraging Australia to invest in other types of military forces while freeing up the enormous resources that would otherwise be consumed in the quest to learn how to operate and maintain these complex platforms. This approach is already in use between the US and its NATO partners and other allies for certain naval capabilities, including SSNs, aircraft carriers and amphibious ships. To go ahead with parallel SSN-related pathway investments in the United States and Australia would result in inefficiencies that have been avoided elsewhere. Instead, the report suggested that Australia invest in long-range anti-ship missiles, which could enter Australian service within the next several years, far sooner than the SSNs. The report's authors also suggested an Australian buy-in to the US's B-21 bomber program, an option that the *DSR*'s authors considered but decided against.[61] Of lesser note, the CRS also touched on the increased risk of a technology security breach as well as the consequences for America's reputation if Australia was to have an accident with one of its American-made SSNs.

Offsetting the potential problems that the SSN transfer might generate was the positive messaging a Pillar I approval would send to China if Congress moved quickly on the transfer authorisation. CRS analysts suggested that selling SSNs to Australia would send China a strong signal, thereby enhancing the deterrence of potential aggression. It would also underscore the collective determination of the AUKUS partners to counter China's military modernisation. In addition, the deterrent value in Australia having its own fleet of SSNs would be greater because it would force China to consider a second decision-making centre in its calculations of operations in the Indo-Pacific, assuming that the Australian boats had the capability to operate independently. That Congress approved the SSN sale suggests that its members considered the deterrence signal sent to China to be a net benefit, even when set against the other issues the CRS analysts raised.[62]

Conclusion

For Australia's entire national history, defence policy has been singularly focused on obtaining the protection of a great power partner. It is also without question that Australia has been remarkably successful at maintaining this policy. Fortunately for Australia, it is also true that the policy of dependency has never been tested. Australia has always been and remains one of the safest countries in the world, distant from traditional global hot spots.

AUKUS, the latest update to Australia's security arrangement, sits within the comfort zone of the country's political leaders. It does little to change the existing equation of Australian security, especially since the eventual price tag is unknown. Australia's political leaders acted in a manner most likely to keep things the same. Australia seems to recognise only one possible defence setting.

The chapters that follow focus on the defence possibilities that have *not* been considered. Australia is not without attractive alternative options when it comes to the provision of national security. That Australia's leaders must contend with a worsening security environment is beyond dispute, and there are serious threats that the nation must protect itself from. Subsequent chapters will identify and evaluate the threats, and outline how to meet them, for the first time in Australia's history, without dependency.

2

AUSTRALIA'S THREAT ENVIRONMENT

DEFENCE POLICY EXISTS IN the context of a state's perception of a potential threat or threats. Once a state's leaders construct an understanding of the threats they face, they can take steps to mitigate the danger or dangers they must deal with. After all, it is the need for security that brings a people together to form a state (or a tribe, clan and so on). It is also why a people accept a leadership class which they entrust with the task of providing the security they desire. Therefore, the most important responsibility Australia's politicians have is to provide for the security of the Australian people. Australia's politicians accomplish this task through the establishment of a defence policy. For a defence policy to be viable the government must also allocate the funds needed to create the capabilities required, for without an appropriate amount of money the policy is an illusion, and merely an opportunity for media announcements that are divorced from reality. For the Australian government, the primary organisation charged with obtaining this security is the Department of Defence through its military arm, the Australian Defence Force (ADF), although other government departments and agencies have important roles to play.

The first step in the provision of security is to understand the nature of the threats the state may face. Without this comprehension, a state's leaders will be unable to prioritise appropriately when they allocate resources for a threat's mitigation. The second step is to assess the degree of actual risk a threat poses to the state and its people. Not all threats represent the same degree of danger – they range from those that are a mere nuisance to ones that are existential. Some threats may be so grave that they exceed a single state's mitigation ability and can only be offset through international collaboration. For example, Australia on its own lacks the ability to prevent a very large meteor from crashing into the earth, but it can work collectively with other nations to detect and divert one.

This chapter will examine the dual threat environment with which Australia's current leaders must contend and assess the degree of risk each represents. The first – the reordering of power in the Western Pacific as a consequence of China's modernisation – is the threat that the government prefers to focus on, and it has received much attention from politicians, military leaders, academics and the security commentariat. The second – climate change and the threat it represents to Australia's interests, if not its very survival as a nation – is under-appreciated by those responsible for the nation's security, and receives from them considerably less consideration. This chapter will establish that a series of governments, both Liberal and Labor, has prioritised focus on a lesser order risk, namely China, to the detriment of addressing the more consequential and likely danger that climate change represents. It will also explore how this failure of realistic interpretation has come about.

I am aware that there are many other potential threats that deserve consideration by Australia's security policy practitioners. These include the growing income gap between the masses of the poor and the wealthy elites; the possibility of another pandemic, including a weaponised one; the global weakening of democracy and resurgence of authoritarianism; and the potential for cyber and artificial intelligence to destabilise essential systems. There is also growing concern about the future stability of the United States, especially given the fickle and autocratic tendencies of President Trump.[1]

The natural world also contains many threats that potentially require mitigation. Some of the most dangerous are the possibility of a large rock smashing into earth, as noted above, a super-volcano eruption – a blast of such a magnitude that it would dwarf all recent eruptions – or a giant tsunami of a force that far exceeds the 2004 Boxing Day event that killed about 230 000 people. Each of these has the potential to kill billions of people if not bring about the end of human civilisation. Each warrants a chapter of its own, exceeding the scope of this modest work. The reader is advised to see the notes for recommended readings on the threat of natural catastrophes.[2]

As someone who came of age during the Cold War, I am well aware that civilisation's destruction as a consequence of a large (or even modest) nuclear exchange remains a threat that we all live with every day, while hoping that day does not come. While the Australian government claims the protection of US extended nuclear deterrence, Australia's capacity to prevent a war's escalation across the nuclear threshold is limited and therefore does not warrant major attention in this work. The security benefit – or liability – of Australia joining the club of nuclear-armed states does warrant consideration, however, and will be examined in chapter 5.

The China threat

The political and military leaders of the United States believe that the greatest menace in the world at present is China and the challenge it represents to America's dominance in the Western Pacific. China is no longer rising – it has risen. It is the second largest economy in the world after the United States, and in fact some commentators think it has already taken the top spot. China's leaders have grown in confidence and capability, and its military, the People's Liberation Army (PLA), has modernised its forces and enhanced its lethality. China's current leader, Xi Jinping, has ruled since 2012 with skill, determination and vision underpinned by a well-developed streak of ruthlessness that has seen him remove rivals and concentrate his own power.

The United States identifies China as 'the only competitor with both the intent to reshape the international order and increasingly, the economic, diplomatic, military and technological power to do it'. China's goal, according to the 2022 US *National Security Strategy*, is to enhance its sphere of influence in the Indo-Pacific and supplant the United States as the world's leading power.[3] By contrast, the US goal for the Indo-Pacific is an environment 'where governments can make their own sovereign choices, consistent with their obligations under international law; and where seas, skies, and other shared domains are lawfully governed'.[4]

China's leaders have not been hesitant to state the extent of their ambitions for their country. In 2017, Xi set the goal of the country's transformation into a great power by mid-century, what he called the realisation of the 'Chinese Dream of national rejuvenation'. A key element in achieving this goal is the building of a powerful military. Xi describes the process in terms of a great struggle, one based on socialist principles but with Chinese characteristics. It is the job of the Chinese Communist Party, Xi demands, to provide the leadership for the people to achieve this dream.[5] Besides providing for the prosperity and security of its people, China believes its destiny is to take responsibility for the region's economic integration as the natural outcome of its rise, as well as becoming the security provider for the Western Pacific, both of which are prerogatives currently enjoyed by the United States.[6] A further component of the Chinese Dream is the reincorporation of Taiwan into the nation. Xi is unambiguous on this point, stating that Taiwan 'must and will be reunited with China'.[7]

An additional dimension to the Chinese Dream is what China's leaders call the 'World Dream'. As China grows in power, it sees as its right a greater involvement in global governance. This includes incorporating Chinese voices into the organisations responsible for such governance, including, one assumes, those bodies established by the United States through which it manages the present global rules-based order.[8] China has not defined what it means by the expression 'World Dream', but it has made a greater effort to advance another idea its leaders call a 'community of common destiny'. In this community, China is the dominant Asian power, the United States is exiled to the Western Hemisphere, and the American alliance system has faded into irrelevance. Regional states would show appropriate deference to Beijing – they would not possess the power to oppose or challenge China's wishes.[9]

US leaders are well aware of the importance of Asia in its assessment of global power. Asia represents approximately 40 per cent of global gross domestic product and is responsible for two-thirds of global growth, meaning that its share of the world's economic output will become larger. In total, Asia's combined economies are larger than that of the United States and are becoming technologically advanced at an impressive pace. From a geopolitical perspective, Asia is the world's most important region. The last thing the United States wants is for a single country to gain a hegemony over the Asian region. If this were to occur, that country would control sufficient resources and economic output to challenge the United States for global dominance.[10] As defence strategist Elbridge A Colby writes, 'the most plausible aspirant to hegemony over one of the world's key regions [is] China'.[11] It is in the interest of the United States to deny a potential rival that opportunity.

To prevent China from achieving control over the Asian landmass and the wider Indo-Pacific, the 2022 US *National Security Strategy* outlines three courses of action:

1. to *invest* in the foundations of our strength at home – our competitiveness, our innovation, our resilience, our democracy;
2. to *align* our efforts with our network of allies and partners, acting with common purpose and in common cause; and
3. to *compete* responsibly with the PRC to defend our interests and build our vision for the future.

Under 'compete' is the entire spectrum of conflict, from actions below the threshold of violence all the way up to state-on-state war. Both of the other courses of action encompass other forms of competition. In support of this strategy the United States plans to reach out to its allies and partners in order to build a coalition of like-minded states whose collective power might deter China from taking military action and prevent it from becoming an Asian hegemon. The *National Security Strategy*'s selling point to regional states is that the construction of an anti-China coalition is the best means by which to assure that they retain the ability to make sovereign decisions for themselves. AUKUS is one example of America enhancing its partnerships against China.[12] The United States already has security treaties or pledges with a number of other Indo-Pacific nations, including Japan, South Korea and the Philippines. However, the security relationship between the United States and its partner Indo-Pacific states contains a paradox. The more powerful the coalition, the less need there will be for major US participation. As Colby notes, 'because of the enormous costs and risks of such a war, the United States has a very great interest in minimizing its involvement in such an effort – or avoiding it entirely'.[13] Colby, a former Pentagon insider and co-lead for the 2018 US *National Security Strategy*, understands that in foreign affairs the first priority for every state is to look after its own interests.

There is no doubt that Australia's leaders also see China as a challenger to the established order and therefore a threat to the nation's interests. The *2020 Defence Strategic Update* recognises the increasing assertiveness of the major powers, including China's 'active pursuit of greater influence in the Indo-Pacific'. It also notes that the strategic competition between the United States and China is the principal driver of the region's strategic dynamics.[14] The 2023 *DSR* continues this theme, identifying the Indo-Pacific as 'the most important geostrategic region in the world'.[15] The *DSR* also highlights China's military build-up, its forceful behaviour in the South China Sea and the challenge it poses to the US-led global rules-based order. As a sub-imperial power within the US Empire, Australia has a vested interest in the continuance of American leadership and economic management across the Indo-Pacific.[16]

It is quite clear that concerns over China occupy a prominent position in the Australian government's security thinking. In an address given at the Australian War Memorial on the theme of defending Australia, Richard Marles mentioned China twenty times, drawing attention to China's military build-up and connecting its creation and militarisation of artificial islands in the South China Sea to the undermining of the global rules-based order. Adding this all together, Marles concludes that China represents 'a significant source of anxiety in respect to our national security'.[17] While speaking to the Lowy Institute, the Prime Minister pursued a similar theme. Albanese pledged that the approach to China was 'careful, methodical and respectful', but also that his government was 'clear-eyed about the situation'. While taking the time to highlight the extent of the nation's trade with China, he warned that 'China does not see itself as a status quo power'. The government's tone harkens back to John Howard's 'be alert but not alarmed' post-9/11 anti-terrorism campaign.[18] Speaking to ASEAN, Penny

Wong, the Minister for Foreign Affairs and Trade, left no doubt that she meant China when she observed that 'we face destabilising, provocative and coercive actions, including unsafe conduct at sea and in the air and militarisation of disputed features'.[19]

In 2013, Hugh White published *The China Choice: Why America Should Share Power*. The book was and remains an important work. White identified three possible options for the United States as it sought to manage the China challenge. They were to:

- compete with China;
- share power with China; or
- concede leadership in Asia to China.

While the focus of the book was on the US–China dynamic, Australia was not very far from White's thoughts. He knew that Australia, tightly bound to the United States, would almost certainly support whatever option America decides to take.[20]

More than ten years on from *The China Choice*, it is clear that the United States has made its choice. It will compete with China in order to determine which nation will dominate the Western Pacific, if not the world. The three points made in the 2022 *National Security Strategy* – invest, align and compete – represent a whole-of-nation pathway whose end point is the continued dominance of the Indo-Pacific by the United States. The United States hopes to garner enough strength from its allies to deter China from initiating military action. War is not its preferred option, but if it proves necessary – for example, in response to a Chinese invasion of Taiwan – the United States will likely wage it.

While Australia is under no threat of invasion itself, the government believes the nation has a stake in the outcome of the US struggle with China for superiority in the Indo-Pacific, as well as in the continued operation of the present global rules-based order. Australia has established its position, both to its great power partner and to China. Marles has stated that 'the consequences of a US–China conflict over Taiwan are so grave that we cannot be passive bystanders', although he does not say what Australia's precise role or contribution would be in such an eventuality.[21]

Of course, it is not possible to know exactly what China intends to do with its increasing economic and military power, or whether or not the United States will continue to push back against the challenge. Yet if China's present trajectory continues and the United States refuses to cede, conflict is the likely result. There already exists a large literature speculating on the possibility of war between the United States and China.[22] What can be said with a greater degree of probability is that Australia, driven by its need to prove commitment and relevancy to the United States, will assist its empire leader in some manner. Only the form this assistance would take remains unknown.

Climate change

As a result of industrialisation, humanity has changed the composition of the earth's atmosphere, initiating a shift in the global climate. Before industrialisation the average concentration of carbon dioxide (CO_2) in the atmosphere was 280 parts per million (ppm). On 11 December 2024, the atmospheric CO_2 had reached 427.85 ppm and there is every certainty that this figure will continue to climb. The atmospheric concentration of methane, nitrous oxide and other greenhouse gases has similarly risen.[23] The CO_2 and other greenhouse gases that humanity has added to the atmosphere have initiated a greenhouse effect, which means the planet retains an excessive amount of heat that drives up the average temperature. Since industrialisation, the average temperature has risen by more than 1.2°C and will continue to increase unless humanity stops adding greenhouse gases to the atmosphere and then takes significant measures to reduce their concentration. The warmest year since records began in 1850 was 2023, and the ten warmest years in the historical record comprise the decade spanning 2014 to 2023.[24]

There is no shortage of signs that the climate is changing. The seas are rising, the ocean is acidifying, the ice is melting, fires are becoming more powerful, storms are becoming more potent, and the animals and plants that cannot adapt rapidly enough to new conditions are dying. Military leaders, particularly in the United States, recognise the threat climate change represents and have said so in public. As early as 2013 the former commander of what was then known as the US Pacific Command, Admiral Samuel Locklear, called climate change the biggest danger in his area of responsibility, a position he reiterated in testimony to the United States Senate Committee on Armed Services.[25] The 2022 *Indo-Pacific Strategy* describes the Command as being at 'the epicentre of the climate crisis'.[26] Locklear's position is not unusual within the military community. Between 2017 and 2019, more than thirty-five senior US Department of Defense officials publicly voiced their concerns over the security implications of climate change.[27] Biden's Secretary of Defense, Lloyd Austin, had continued the pattern by labelling climate change an 'existential threat'.[28] Despite Trump's reversal of policy, demonstrated by actions such as his insistence on eradicating mention of it from US government websites, documents and educational materials, climate change is just as real as ever.

As the world gathered in late 2023 in Dubai for the annual climate summit, the United Nations Secretary General, António Guterres, declared that the 'earth's vital signs are failing: record emissions, ferocious fires, deadly droughts and the hottest year ever'.[29] The following year, in preparation for the next summit at Baku, Guterres acknowledged that the world was approaching irreversible tipping points that would greatly accelerate the impacts of climate change.[30] Guterres was not exaggerating the threat. At the 2015 Paris Summit, the attending states agreed to hold the average temperature rise to 1.5°C above pre-industrial levels by having greenhouse gas emissions peak by 2025 and decline by 43 per cent by 2030. Failing to achieve this objective would irretrievably change the climate in ways that would risk the survival of humanity, as well as many other species.[31] It is cause for considerable concern that some scientists, including James Hansen who is called the godfather of climate science, believe that 1.5°C has already been breached. According to the European Union's Copernicus Climate Change Service, humanity's crossing of the 1.5°C barrier is imminent. It reported the average temperature increase over pre-industrial levels for 2023 as 1.498°C.[32] If this is repeated in 2025, then humanity is truly heading into a dangerous unknown.

When a US Secretary of Defense identifies climate change as an existential threat, everyone should take notice. However, the Dubai and Baku climate meetings, like its predecessors, ended with its participating nations – including Australia – voicing many pledges but not committing to meaningful action.[33] When he spoke at CSIS in Washington DC in 2022, Marles included in his address a few words on the danger climate change represented for humanity. He also claimed that Australia was ready to tackle the challenge, saying:

> One of the biggest concerns we hear is the threat of climate change. It's a threat from which no one and no country is immune. And it is a threat that demands action. The Albanese Government wants to make climate change a pillar of the Alliance. Because it is clear climate change is a national security issue. When you stand on the shores of our Pacific neighbours, as I have, you understand the intense vulnerability felt by those living on small islands. The Pacific Islands Forum, of which Australia is a member, has been consistent in declaring climate change as the single greatest threat to livelihoods in our neighbourhood – it is an existential threat. The Forum has also been consistent in calling for the countries of the Pacific – including Australia – to work together in response. Under Prime Minister Albanese, Australia will lift its weight.[34]

Presumably, Marles said this with a straight face since Australia is one of the countries most guilty of failing to match words with action. Thus, because of a lack of will on the part of the leaders of the critical nations to take action, the only outcome possible is a global catastrophe which will result in the collapse of many states and the death of unimaginable numbers of people.

Australia occupies a relatively safe part of the world, well removed from centres of danger and turmoil such as the Middle East or sub-Saharan Africa. Few present-day Australians have experience with the collapse of their society, nor understand the consequences for their survival that such an event holds. Climate change scientists and climate change communicators tend to focus on the dangerous effect climate change is having on the intensity of storms, or the risk posed to coastal living from rising seas. In the summer of 2019–20 more than 24 million hectares of Australia burnt during months of fires. A CSIRO study found that over the last thirty years, fires had increased enormously in size – between the periods 1988–2001 and 2002–18, the average size of a fire had grown by 350 per cent. When the 2019–20 fires are included, that figure rises to 800 per cent. In addition, places that did not usually experience fire were now burning. CSIRO researchers concluded that the worsening fire seasons were consistent with climate change.[35]

The fires, despite their horror, did not cause the Australian state to collapse. Other populations will not be so lucky. In 2023, the governments of Australia and Tuvalu concluded the Falepili Union Treaty. The treaty gives the people of Tuvalu the right to settle in Australia when their country becomes uninhabitable as a result of climate change. The Tuvalu government believes it will literally disappear under rising seas and has negotiated a refuge for its people.[36] What Australia expects will happen to Tuvalu will not be uncommon. Climate change not only causes changes in the environment, but it compounds these changes as they intersect in unpredictable ways. Consequently, climate change is known as a 'threat multiplier'. What this means is that climate change causes a worsening of existing conditions which overwhelm the ability of a state to manage. At some point, many states will run out of resources, money, expertise or resolve and will no longer be able to meet the needs of the people. CNA, the Washington DC-based think-tank that was formally known as the Center for Navy Analysis, believes that climate change will exacerbate existing stressors to the point that they exceed the ability of many governments to manage.[37] What follows is collapse.

A brief examination of essential resources highlights how climate change brings about societal collapse. The most critical human needs are, of course, food and water. Any shortage of these necessities is likely to cause unrest, destabilisation and finally societal collapse, which leads to a people's greater willingness to resort to force to safeguard and secure its needs. Those who grow or gather food know that the water needed to irrigate crops must arrive at a particular place, at a particular time and in a certain quantity, while fishers need to know where the fish will be at a specific time of the year, and pastoralists need to know when they have to move their herds to different ranges. Agriculturalists produce the food needed to feed the more than eight billion people on the planet. However, climate change will destabilise how the environment generates the resources humans rely on and their predictability. Instead of a stable climate, humanity will have to deal with a highly unstable one. The effect will be a reduction in food production and an increasingly hungry planet. The outcome will be greater violence as humans choose to fight for what they need. A 2016 intelligence report produced by the US National Intelligence Council anticipated that climate change will have 'significant direct and indirect social, economic, political, and security implications during the next 20 years'.[38]

A report produced by the US Office of the Director of National Intelligence raised the alarm:

> Many countries important to the United States are vulnerable to natural resource shocks that degrade economic development, frustrate attempts to democratize, raise the risk of regime-threatening instability, and aggravate regional tensions. Extreme weather events ... will increasingly disrupt food and energy markets, exacerbating state weakness, forcing human migrations, and triggering riots, civil disobedience, and vandalism. Criminal or terrorist elements can exploit any of these weaknesses to conduct illicit activity and/or recruitment and training. Social disruptions are magnified in growing urban areas where information technology transmits grievances to larger ... audiences and relatively small events can generate significant effects across regions or the world.[39]

The predicted instability brought about by climate change will overwhelm the coping capacity of many societies, particularly fragile ones. Even if the Australian government is able to handle the strain, it will need to deal with a destabilised region that will feature mass migration, pervasive unrest and widespread violence.

While climate change is an environmental event, it is also an issue for national security, one that will strike all aspects of societal organisation. For Australians, the increased risk of the flooding of one's coastal holiday house may see the price of insurance soar, but for most of the world's population, particularly in less wealthy countries, the risks from climate change are life or death in nature. There is a correlation between an unstable climate and human misery. In a destabilising future, Australia and its military can expect to become involved in regional wars with greater frequency, if only as peacekeepers separating multiple adversaries. These wars are also likely to be more deadly and decisive as people see no choice other than to fight for survival. Unless the world's major greenhouse gas economies, of which Australia is one, rapidly reduce emissions, the future world looks like a more violent one. To date, unfortunately, the international political will to move quickly to lower emissions has been lacking, and the Trump administration's advocacy for an increase in fossil fuel production means humanity is even more likely to experience the full fury of a climate change future.

Considering the risk

Soon after the start of 2024, the staff of the *Bulletin of the Atomic Scientists* (henceforth *Bulletin*) performed their annual ritual of resetting the Doomsday Clock for the year. The *Bulletin* created the clock in 1947, at the start of the Cold War, as an indicator of the world's vulnerability to human-induced catastrophe. For 2024, they kept the clock at ninety seconds to midnight, the same as the previous year, representing the closest to catastrophe humanity had ever been to that point. In making its determination, the organisation's Science and Security Board highlighted a number of grave concerns they had, any of which could bring the human experiment to an end: the potential use of nuclear weapons in Ukraine and elsewhere, an ominous climate change outlook, evolving biological threats including weaponised diseases, and the unknown dangers posed by artificial intelligence.[40]

The Doomsday Clock is a general representation of humanity's prospect for self-extermination in the coming year, with a nuclear exchange being the quickest way to end our future. While the Doomsday Clock should be seen as a warning of imminent extinction, it can also be seen as a beacon of hope. It is possible to move away from the brink: after the end of the Cold War the *Bulletin* moved it to seventeen minutes to midnight as a result of the lessening of tension between the United States and Russia. What this suggests is that it is possible for a state to implement policies that reduce the danger it faces from a threat and provide greater security for its people.

The first step a government needs to take is to establish a defence policy that identifies the threat or threats the nation faces.

The *Bulletin*, being an organisation not a state, has a global perspective. The Australian government must be more specific in order to focus its limited resources on the most critical threats to the nation's future. Not every threat represents the same degree of danger – it may affect one or more states, and no two nations will have an equal quantity of resources with which to mitigate it.

The Australian government releases periodic defence policy documents that identify what it believes are the threats against which it must take action. These documents also justify the government's allocation of money and other resources for the threat's mitigation – a form of public accountability. The government's threat perception is clear from the 2023 *DSR*. It allocates to climate change a bit more than a page, in a document of more than 100 pages, and the text summarises what Defence will not do in future climate emergencies. Basically, the *DSR* concludes a climate change role for the ADF is not its job. The inclusion of the section is to make a case for not employing Defence assets to mitigate climate change because the ADF is funded to fight wars. The section's authors have completely misunderstood what national security actually means and have failed to imagine the relevance to Australia and the ADF of the conflicts a destabilised climate will spawn across the region. Still, while representing only about 1 per cent of the document's length, that many words are without precedent in a Defence strategic policy document – only a few years earlier, from the author's personal experience, it was hazardous to one's career to utter the words 'climate change' in the corridors of the Department of Defence.[41]

There is no doubt that China is a serious threat to American interests. China's challenge to the US-led rules-based order is real, as is its potential to displace the United States and become an Asian hegemon. While there is little chance that China intends to invade, conquer and rule Australia, it is entirely possible that it may impose a rules-based order that is less beneficial to Australia than the present one or make demands on Australia that the government and its citizens feel they have no option other than to agree to.

Yet, for a state, the most serious dangers are those that threaten its very existence. If such dangers are left unaddressed, the state's leaders have failed at their most important responsibility they owe to the people they represent – the provision of security. As with a war between two nuclear-armed states, climate change is a global existential risk. Climate change has the potential to so destabilise civilisation that it could cause widespread social collapse, myriad intra- and inter-state wars and the deaths of billions of people.

Unfortunately, the Australian government is largely focusing its national security policy attention on China to the detriment of a focus on climate change. When expending funds, the ADF does so on capabilities that are designed for a war against China as a member of a US-led coalition. Through AUKUS, the government is dedicating scarce resources to develop a suite of new advanced warfighting technologies: a policy, research and funding effort that is not matched by efforts to mitigate climate change. Further showing its threat preference, in early 2024, the government released its plan for the RAN's future surface combatant fleet which authorised a doubling of its size compared with the previous government's plan. The report emphasises the need to boost the RAN's 'air defence, long-range strike, presence and anti-submarine warfare capabilities'.[42] While it did not specifically mention China, there is little doubt what sparked this fleet build-up or against whom all this firepower would be directed. Climate change did not receive a mention in either the Department of Defence's media release or the full report, nor did it get a promise of additional funds. Any suggestion of climate change funding or preparation remained unfulfilled in the 2024 *Integrated Investment Plan* and the 2024 *National Defence Strategy*. When following the money, the allocation to anti-China defence capabilities illustrates just where the government's national security priority lies.

Australia is in the uncomfortable position of facing two different threats at the same time. In the annals of international policy this is unfortunate, but not unprecedented, even for Australia. For example, while Australian troops fought the Boers alongside British and other Commonwealth forces in South Africa, another contingent sailed for China to help suppress the Boxer Rebellion. For a considerable period, Australia's participation in the wars in Afghanistan and Iraq was simultaneous, while at the same time the government continued to address a third threat – the possibility of a terrorist attack on Australian soil. Of course, while these military operations were underway the international community was looking for the means to deal with another threat, climate change. States often have to manage multiple concurrent threats.

This is not an argument to prioritise the guaranteed danger of climate change and to ignore the potential threat of China. Australia will need to consider both and provide the resources needed for their mitigation. Still, it is very odd that Australia's political leaders have decided to focus nearly exclusively on the threat that they prefer rather than the one that represents the greatest danger. Such partiality requires some explanation.

An immature definition of security

The definition of security that Australia's political leaders and policy-makers practise can be politely described as immature. One might also say it is unimaginative, because it is unable to appreciate national security threats that do not fall within narrow and predetermined boundaries. The threat types Australia chooses to recognise as a risk to national security are those that originate from another state or sub-state actor, to the exclusion of other kinds. This is unfortunate because the responsibility of Australia's leaders to provide for the security of their citizens should not be selectively applied. All security threats warrant mitigation, if they pose a danger to Australians.

China poses a national security threat that the government can understand and accept. Climate change does not fit into the same template, even though it should since it is expected to destabilise states around the world, with the fragile states that inhabit the Global South being at particular risk from climate change events. Overwhelmed by repeated climate shocks, governance collapse is likely followed by a return to the brutal state of nature that Thomas Hobbes describes in *Leviathan*.[43] While the decision for war will remain a choice, desperate times will compel people to act. Climate change will drive conflicts across the spectrum of societal organisation, whether they be launched by states, tribes, clans or mobs. Yet the federal government prefers to view the risk from climate change as being one of larger and more frequent fires, floods and cyclones, not one of mass migration, internal displacement and regional conflicts. In other words, climate change is considered only as a threat from the natural world, and thus mostly a matter for Australia's state-based emergency services. Australia's policy-makers must urgently expand their understanding of what security means.

Hindering such an expanded understanding is that to do so would require going against the defence narrative articulated by the United States, as well as challenging the policy preferences of Australia's fossil fuel industries. Even though the United States has a much more mature understanding of climate change risks than Australia, the menace posed by a stronger and more confident China to the US-led global order is the one that garners most of its attention. It is a possible war with China that it is preparing to fight, not the likely climate-provoked wars that are to come. It would be uncharacteristically courageous for Australia's political leaders to take a contrary position and make climate change their priority national security narrative.

To move aggressively against climate change, the Australian government would also have to break faith with some of Australia's most profitable exporters: the fossil fuel industries represented by coal and natural gas. Despite the necessity to reduce greenhouse gas emissions, Australia continues to provide subsidies and favourable tax treatments for fossil fuel extraction and funds the building of fossil fuel infrastructure. The Albanese government has opened Australian waters to oil and gas exploration and has endorsed the opening of new mines. Mining has driven the Australian economy for decades and, therefore, its privileges are well entrenched in government policy settings. A study from The Australia Institute shows that in 2021 Australia had seventy-two new coal mines and forty-four gas and oil projects under development, which if they reached production would double Australia's existing output of these minerals. Contrary to the International Energy Agency's assessment that there can be no new investment in fossil fuels if humanity is to meet its greenhouse gas emissions target, the Australian government sees less risk to itself by continuing to protect the coal and gas industry.[44]

Australia's use of an inadequate definition for national security has serious consequences. First, it encourages the selection of a lesser threat as the main focus of defence policy. Second, it contributes to encouraging the United States to maintain its own secondary-risk threat narrative, while allowing status quo–vested fossil fuel industries to have a negative influence on the nation's future security. A broadening of the definition would enable the government to overcome these deficiencies.

The probability factor

To mitigate the myriad threats a state may face it is also critical to take into account the probability of an event's occurrence. Those responsible for planning a state's defence need to have a sense of how likely an event is, in order to make sound decisions that are in the national interest. A threat that is identified as the most dangerous and most likely demands more of a government's focus than threats that are less dangerous or less probable. The only case in which it is appropriate, at least in the short term, to ignore a very dangerous threat is if the possibility of its occurrence is so remote as to not warrant the allocation of any attention other than monitoring.

Usually, there are no guarantees when estimating whether a future event will occur. The future is unknown and there are many factors that support human decision-making. Because humans are complex beings in which emotion and irrationality play a part in decisions, the one eternal truth about predicting the future is that those predictions are likely to be wrong. However, there are exceptions. Some future threats can be precisely predicted because they are based not on human actions but on the physical laws that govern the operation of the earth, solar system and universe. For example, astronomers scan the sky for large asteroids and comets whose trajectory might collide with that of our planet. When astronomers detect a new object, they can calculate whether or not its course will intersect with the earth. During the age of humans, impacts have occurred, but fortunately they have been below the level of an extinction level event, such as the 1908 Tunguska incident in Siberia. Clearly major collisions have occurred in the distant past. Sixty-six million years ago an asteroid struck the planet in the Yucatán area of Mexico. The consequences of the impact brought the age of the dinosaurs to an end.

By changing the composition of the atmosphere, humanity has altered the climate. At this point, there is nothing humans can do to stop earth systems from performing in a different manner than previously. This is locked in: the climate change threat is a certainty. It is occurring and will only become worse, particularly if humanity does not rapidly bring its emission of greenhouse gases to zero. Moreover, even if humanity was to reduce emissions to zero tomorrow, climate change would continue to worsen because of the ongoing effect of increased presence of greenhouse gases in the atmosphere. It is too late for humanity to avoid the pain of climate change – it is the full extent of the pain that remains to be decided.

By contrast, the threat that China will overturn the US-led global rules-based order, displace America in the Western Pacific, and become the Asian hegemon, is not a certainty. It is not possible to state with any degree of accuracy the probability of this occurring, because so many of the factors involved are human-based, and predicting an adversary's political intentions and military capabilities is always, at best, an inexact process. All that can be said is the realisation of the China threat is less than 100 per cent and therefore, not as certain as that of climate change. In addition, it is also impossible to predict when China will become a sated power. China's leaders may be satisfied with only the reincorporation of Taiwan and abandon any grander ambitions they might hold, at least for now. In addition, international security analyst Allan Behm has made the case that the true threat to Australia's security in the US–China contest is the collapse of America as a result of internal political and social tensions, an event that is looking more likely since he penned his observation.[45]

In recent decades, China has grown immensely in economic and military power. The PLA has modernised rapidly and is now fielding advanced military systems. In some areas, such as hypersonic missiles, China is ahead of the United States. In a 2021 test, China's D-41 hypersonic missile circumnavigated the globe. The PLA also fields missiles that are able to hold US targets at risk out to and beyond American bases on Guam. The PLA Navy is posed to overtake the USN in several metrics of maritime power and the decline of US relative naval strength will be almost impossible to reverse.[46] While it is difficult to predict a potential adversary's future actions and simplistic to expect the pattern of the past to be the pattern of the future, there is similarly no reason to expect that China's continued growth is guaranteed. In fact, there are signs that suggest China is destined for a sharp fall as it faces numerous domestic challenges. These include:

- a sluggish economy;
- a debt crisis that affects major corporations and provincial/local governments;
- an ageing population in a nation that lacks a social security backstop;
- a toxic environment that is unable to provide citizens with clean air to breathe and water to drink;
- a surplus of males, numbering in the tens of millions, for whom there are no female partners; and
- a leadership that continues to suppress any expression that threatens the place of the Chinese Communist Party.[47]

In addition, there are a host of longstanding practices that can affect China's growth trajectory, including the oppression of ethnic minorities, the denial of information to the population, and an institutionalised violation of human rights.

Nor are all of the variables in the Western Pacific power balance on China's side of the ledger. The United States has problems of its own, perhaps the most significant being the willingness of a large number of Americans to embrace autocratic leadership. At the 2024 US election Americans decided to return Donald Trump to the presidency. His unpredictability, narcissism and admiration for dictators could lead to massive changes to American foreign policy. He has already threatened to withdraw from NATO, thereby ending a US policy that has successfully maintained peace in Western Europe for seventy-five years. This is a president, after all, who once yelled, 'I don't give a shit about NATO'.[48] The well-regarded commentator Max Boot believed that if Trump returned to the White House he would destroy the US-led world order, the very thing Australia's political leaders have long attached themselves to and seek to perpetuate.[49] Boot's prediction seems to be coming true as Trump turns against allies and friends alike, while currying favour with repugnant regimes such as Putin's Russia. It would be extraordinarily naïve to assume that Trump's 'America first' agenda, and his anti-democratic compulsions would not see him discard ANZUS as well.[50] His hostility to environmental protection and climate change mitigation has been proven by the actions of his previous administration, which included withdrawing the United States from the 2015 Paris Agreement, an act he repeated shortly after his second inauguration.

The United States is placing a big bet that nothing will derail China from an inexorable rise that will result in a direct confrontation in Asia for dominance. Australia is placing a major bet too, that it will not be abandoned if the United States turns its back on the international community and withdraws inwardly. The point here in regards to China, and to the United States, is that current power trajectories may change. The two powers may even come to an accommodation by non-military means. By contrast, when it comes to climate change the prediction of the future is on much more solid ground – humanity can expect a very rough ride ahead as it attempts to adapt to a new climatic age. Australia's leaders would be wise when deciding upon security policy to give as much attention to the guaranteed existential threat as they do to their favoured but less certain and less dire one.

The neglect of strategy

Australia is not a strategy-minded nation. Its political and military leaders have rarely needed or sought to act at the strategic level of war. Instead, the Australian military has excelled at the tactical level – the waging of battle. The Australian political and military classes' lack of knowledge of and experience with the development and conduct of strategy helps to explain the government's prioritisation of China's threat ahead of that posed by climate change.

As a small state in league with a great power, Australia rarely has the opportunity to influence the strategic objectives of the coalition to which it belongs. For example, in the Second World War the United States did not consult Australia on how it intended to conduct the war against Japan. In fact, in early 1942, when the American general Douglas MacArthur arrived in Melbourne, Prime Minister John Curtin handed him control of all Australian military forces in the South-West Pacific Theatre. Additionally, MacArthur became Curtin's military advisor. In combination, this meant that a foreign general was responsible for the defence of Australia.[51] MacArthur made it clear to his Australian hosts that he had no personal interest in Australia's fate in the war. For him, Australia's sole utility was as a springboard from which to attack and defeat the Japanese. The interests of the two countries aligned in a common enemy, but for MacArthur, and rightly so, America's interests always came first.[52]

Since the end of the Second World War, Australia has participated in numerous wars, always as a minor partner among a coalition of states led by either the United States or the United Kingdom. In every case, Australia has committed as little military force as possible and its presence has made absolutely no difference to the war's outcome. The latest request from the United States to join a maritime protection mission in the Red Sea against Yemen-based Houthi militants was met with a contribution of eleven additional staff to the Middle East to help with the operation. This was subsequently raised to sixteen and given the name Operation Hydranth. Australia decided not to send a ship.[53] The primary purpose of Australia's contribution to all these operations was alliance management not warfighting. The presence of the Australian flag was enough to satisfy the Americans. Consequently, Australia has never provided enough forces to warrant a role in the higher direction of these wars.

While the United States was an accomplished practitioner of strategy in the Second World War and throughout the Cold War, following the collapse of the Soviet Union America's leaders distanced themselves from its art. According to historian Andrew Bacevich, the victory over the Soviet Union ushered in a period of US militarism dominated by a 'heedless absence of self-restraint, with shallow moralistic impulses overriding thoughtful strategic analysis'.[54] The concept of American exceptionalism, which has a long history, is the belief that the United States is a unique and morally superior nation. Of course, this concept is one of faith, not reality, as any examination of the inequities that plague the United States shows a country that is fractured by internal divisions.[55] Yet, facts do not deter those in leadership positions from accepting that the United States has the responsibility and right to spread its values globally, by force if necessary. A faith in its own exceptionalism and, for many, a deep conviction that God has given the United States unique prerogatives drives a military policy that allows US leaders to rationalise the use of force in the first instance. Thus, the United States' sense of its own invincibility has replaced any need for the serious consideration of strategy and the setting of achievable war aims.[56]

For Australia, the art of strategy-making begins and ends by demonstrating its willingness to help the United States when called upon. Nick Minchin, the finance minister in Howard's government, believed that:

> Where there's an opportunity to show our bonafides in a genuine way we ought to take it – given reasonable risk assessments – because there are not many occasions on which we can legitimately do that and because ... it's not a matter of Australia ever being in a situation where we come to America's rescue. It's always going to be the other way around.[57]

When your objective is to demonstrate to your protector your allegiance, there is little need to go into the finer details of who you are fighting, why and to what end. Robert Hill, the Australian defence minister from 2001 to 2006, observed that one of the things that struck him about getting into the wars in Afghanistan and Iraq was 'how little [we] knew about the country and the influences in the country'.[58] If you go to war in a state of ignorance, it is impossible to develop and carry through an achievable strategy.

As long as being seen to be helping is the limit of a nation's ambitions, its leaders will never have the need to nor the interest in conducting strategy. This means Australia has to be content with following the lead of other nations in setting policy objectives and allocating the means to achieve goals. The primacy of the China threat is the result.

Conclusion

Thucydides, the doyen of international relations, identified three causes for war. They are 'fear, honour and interest', and though he lived about 2600 years ago his pithy analysis remains as relevant today as when he wrote it.[59] The threats posed by both China and climate change easily fit within Thucydides' war-causing factors. That said, they are not equal – different threats rarely are.

When faced with multiple threats, a state's leaders will usually prioritise the dangers they face. In the situation that Australia presently faces, the government has decided that China is the priority, even though as a risk it is neither as likely nor dangerous as climate change. The government has come to this conclusion because of the inadequacy of its threat assessment process. The author does not maintain that China is *not* a threat to Australia's interests, only that it is the lesser of the two. The China threat does require the government's attention and mitigation but it cannot be at the expense of the greater risk of climate change. Therefore, Australia needs to broaden its definition of what constitutes a national security threat so that it can also accommodate climate change in its defence policy.

3

DESIGNING AUSTRALIA'S FUTURE DEFENCE POLICY

AUSTRALIA FACES TWO MAIN threats that the government must manage if the nation is to be secure. As established in chapter 2, these threats are the potential for climate change to destabilise the region and spark inter- and intra-state wars, and the prospect of China becoming an Asian hegemon and overturning the US-led global rules-based order. Of the two, climate change is the more dangerous as it is an existential threat not just to Australia but to humanity more generally. China, while a threat on its own, is a hazard of a lower order, at least for Australia. China's neighbours, particularly Taiwan, face a different security situation. The current Australian government and its predecessors have consistently preferred to invest in addressing the China threat while ignoring that of climate change. Although this preference is in keeping with traditional Australian defence policy, it is based on a flawed foundation and leads to imprudent solutions. A balance that mitigates both threats must be struck.

One of the objectives of this chapter is to outline a defence philosophy – the Strategic Defensive – that is able to address both of these major threats to Australian security. When it comes to national security Australia's political leaders cannot afford to bury their heads in the sand if faced by a threat that does not appeal to them. The nation deserves a solution that mitigates the risks posed by both climate change and China. The Strategic Defensive will do that.

The Strategic Defensive will require some changes to the ADF's force structure and equipment, but most of the modifications fall within the remit of defence 'attitude' or 'posture'. Government and military leaders will need to think differently on the nation's defence than they presently do. Cancelling acquisition programs and modifying force structures is relatively easy to accomplish – the ADF does it all the time. The real challenge in force development and war preparation is getting leaders to think differently from the way they have become accustomed. As military theorist BH Liddell Hart observed, the 'only thing harder than getting a new idea into the military mind is to get an old one out', words that can also apply to Australia's political class.[1] The following chapters will consider the intellectual, organisational and equipment requirements that will enable Australia's adoption of the Strategic Defensive.

Defining Australia as a nation state

Most Australians see themselves as a fun-loving, sport-obsessed nation of natural larrikins. The more serious-minded view Australia as a liberal democracy with ties of tradition and history to Britain and a natural affinity to the United States as mutual members of the Anglosphere. The original inhabitants of Australia have their own ideas and might rightly refer to the members of the now dominant culture as invaders. Perhaps the most famous description of Australia was Donald Horne's 'the lucky country', although he did not mean the phrase as a compliment.[2] As this work deals with national security and military affairs, the most useful descriptor for Australia's place in the world would be a 'status quo power'.

A status quo power is a state that is sated. Australia's people are happy with what they have, in geopolitical terms, and have no desire to take anything from anyone else. The Australian people do not lust after someone else's territory, resources or even status. Australia is a contented nation and other states have no reason to fear any hostility or avarice from it.

In part, this sense of satisfaction is due to Australia being a very wealthy nation whose territory is able to provide what is needed to support a consumerist first-world lifestyle. What Australia's territory cannot supply is easily obtained on the international market through the globalised trade network of which it is a part. Therefore, for Australians the best international relations outcome to any crisis is for the world to remain just as it is, and their government would similarly prefer no challenge to the existing order.

Obviously, Australia has not always been a status quo state. The arrival of the British in 1788 ushered in a period of aggression towards and extermination of the indigenous population and the colonisation of the land, a process that was similar in conduct and outcome to other European and American conquests that took place elsewhere during roughly the same period. The European settlers took the continent by force and displaced the existing inhabitants from their land.

In contrast to Australia, the United States and China are aggressive nations that seek to impose their wishes on lesser states. While neither China nor the United States has designs on each other's territory, they display aggression in other ways. China wants to bring Taiwan back under its control and to supplant the United States as the dominant power in the region. In brief, China is a revisionist state whose goal is to become the Asian hegemon with the power to set the rules for how its part of the world operates. The United States, having previously established its dominance, wants to deny

China its goals. In this particular context, the aim of the United States is to maintain the status quo – yet keeping the status quo should not suggest a policy of non-aggression. After all, policing an empire often requires the use of force.

That Australia, a status quo state, is a close ally of the United States, an aggressor state, does require some explanation. In a potentially hostile world, Australia has traditionally assessed itself as unable to protect its own interests, and even its territory, without assistance. Therefore, it positions itself as a sub-imperial state in a great power's empire. The great power maintains trade arrangements from which Australia generates much of its wealth, while also providing a national security assurance. Australia's leaders have consistently been untroubled by their nation being a status quo power within aggressive empires. In fact, it is a position that they actively embrace and seek to perpetuate.

Allan Behm of The Australia Institute summed up Australia's place in the global order thus: '[it] has been quick to join with imperial and quasi-imperial powers in global action to preserve the imperial status quo or to defeat challengers to that status quo'.[3] The government does recognise and accept that it is a status quo state. In her 2023 address to the National Press Club, Penny Wong stated that Australia does 'not want to see any unilateral change in the status quo'. She continued, moreover, that 'the status quo was superior to any alternative'. Wong made it clear that the state attempting to upset the status quo was China, by employing its power to coerce its neighbours, particularly Taiwan. Wong also commented on Australia's explicit support of the United States and its objectives. She highlighted that it was in the region's interest that it operated by standards, rules and norms in which 'a larger country does not determine the fate of a smaller country; where each country can pursue its own aspirations, its own prosperity'. She continued that the rivalry between China and the United States was 'nothing less than a contest over the way our region and our world work'.[4] Speaking in Washington, Albanese also saw China's desire to refashion the global rules-based order as an attempt to destroy the status quo.[5] From their own words, there is only one conclusion: Australia's leaders would prefer to continue to reside in a world in which the status quo takes precedence, the US rules-based order remains in effect and China does not become the Asian hegemon. For Australia, to support the United States is to support the status quo.

Admitting weakness

Australia is a second order power when compared to the states jostling to dominate the Indo-Pacific. This status is a consequence of several factors but primarily due to Australia's small population, large land mass and the size of its economy when juxtaposed with other Indo-Pacific states. Its military weakness is not just due to its lesser population and economy, however. It is a result of deliberate government policy. Australia offsets its relative military weakness by leveraging the military strength of its great power protector. The government assumes that any potential adversary will factor in the support the United States will provide to Australia in its risk/benefit calculation of whether or not to go to war. This has the effect of making Australia a bigger problem for any state considering an attack and may cause the aggressor to hesitate to act or to rethink and abandon its plans.

Economic power is what states use to create military power. There was a time when Australia's economy dominated the region, but that is no longer the case. China's economy is now ten times the size of Australia's and the disparity is only expected to grow: in 2023 China's Gross Domestic Product (GDP) was US$17.8 trillion versus US$1.72 trillion for Australia.[6] Moreover, the PLA is modernising at an impressive rate as it incorporates the latest weapon systems and military technologies into its arsenal and way of war. There is also no comparison between the two countries' populations: China's is fifty-four times the size of Australia's. By such critical measurements, Australia is clearly the weaker of the two and it is difficult to see the balance of economic power ever changing in its favour.[7]

When the government invests in defence capabilities, its design principle is to build a force that is optimised to fight as a junior member in a US-led coalition on a US-generated operation. Possessing military forces whose primary purpose is to defend Australia on their own is not a major concern. This design principle is longstanding. When Australia looked to the United Kingdom for protection, its military forces reflected imperial requirements.

The design principle of fighting alongside US forces is made more explicit by the fact that the ADF has forsaken specialist needs that are essential to the ability to wage modern warfare. The result is that in war the US military provides the ADF with a host of essential services and support functions. For example, in the Afghanistan and Iraq wars, Australian forces relied upon the United States for intelligence, close air support, artillery fire, transport, the evacuation of casualties and a host of other activities. Even fuel and water came through the US supply system. It was the same in the Vietnam War where the Australians fighting in Phuoc Tuy Province received much of their support from the US supply system.[8]

The primary design principle behind the ADF's force structure and its future development is to be interoperable with the US military. The Royal Australian Air Force is essentially a wing of the US Air Force, the Royal Australian Navy can smoothly fit into a US Navy task force, and units of the Australian Army can easily operate under American command alongside US ground forces. Despite such existing high levels of reliance, the Australian government wants the ADF to achieve even greater integration with the US military system. When he addressed the CSIS in 2022, Marles told the audience that one of his goals was for the ADF to 'move beyond interoperability to interchangeability', and he wanted to reach the point where the militaries of the two nations could 'operate seamlessly together at speed'.[9] AUKUS is a part of this endeavour, and an aspect of the agreement is a pledge by Australia and the United States to work towards greater integration. While the government's policy direction enhances the ability of the ADF to work with the US military, it does so at the cost of not being able to conduct independent operations.

It is commonplace for Australian politicians and academics to refer to Australia as a 'middle power', thereby conferring upon the country a relatively high degree of status in the world's hierarchy of states. This descriptor might carry weight in foreign policy circles, but in the military sphere the term 'middle power' is a nonsense. In war, power is relative, and great states have the resources with which to generate a higher quantity of combat power than do smaller ones. While a great power may not always win against a lesser opponent – for example the failure of the United States in Vietnam – it is generally favoured. Because of the relative nature of military power there could be circumstances in which Australia is a great power. For example, matched against the military might of Tuvalu or Tonga, Australia is the great power. However, against China, Australia is not a middle power – it is a small power. The reality is that it is only due to its military dependence on the United States that Australia is able to act above its proper station. It would be wise for Australians to understand their true place in the world when confronted by those that may intend to do the nation harm.

The only area in which Australia enjoys a military advantage is its geography. Australia is an island continent and consequently does not share a land border with any potential adversaries. This means that any aggressor would have to project power across the sea in order to reach Australia. The need to cross water greatly complicates an aggressor's offensive movement because it necessitates a large amphibious effort, the employment of many transport and support vessels and a vulnerable supply line, all of which ADF ships, planes and land-based missiles could interdict. It is true that contemporary long-range strike systems allow an attacker to bombard Australia from a distance, but as the Japanese raid on Darwin showed in the Second World War, bombs alone, short of nuclear ones, are rarely able to coerce a people to concede – greater pressure is required. In his classic account of coercion and aerial bombardment, political scientist Robert Pape concluded that by themselves such attacks are insufficient to make an adversary concede. As an island continent, Australia is a bastion and while it might suffer damage from long-range strikes it is well placed to weather the storm.[10]

An understanding of war

In order to understand the defence policy that Australia needs, it is necessary to have a basic understanding of how military leaders think about war and to define some of the terms they use. It is also critical to understand the purpose of war.

The most effective way for a state to secure its sovereignty is to possess a sound military organisation whose size and capability is sufficient to deter or defeat a potential aggressor. This is not a new idea. It was articulated by Vegetius, a fourth-century Roman writer in his *Epitome of Military Science*. It is worth quoting Vegetius in full:

> Therefore, he who desires peace, let him prepare for war. He who wants victory, let him train soldiers diligently. He who wishes a successful outcome, let him fight with strategy, not at random. No one dares challenge or harm one who he realizes will win if he fights.[11]

While Vegetius's observation is best known for explaining the benefit of being strong, he also has something important to say on the consequences of a state's failure to address its security properly. States that are militarily weak could be seen to invite war because an aggressor has no reason to fear the consequence of an attack.

Thus, when circumstances – including leadership decision-making – leave a state relatively weak, it must be prepared to concede to an aggressor's wishes or, if possible, come to an arrangement with those who might do it harm. In 1940, Denmark chose to concede when confronted by a much stronger Germany. By contrast, during the Peloponnesian War the small island of Milos refused all entreaties to surrender when confronted by the great power Athens and, as a result, was utterly destroyed.

Accommodation is another possibility for the weak, and Finland's performance in the aftermath of its 1939–40 war with the Soviet Union offers a sagacious example. Finland lost the war and while it had to cede some of its territory, it survived as an independent state. That it was able to endure was due to the stiff resistance and resolute will it had offered during the war. Successive Finnish political leaders understood the limits of their independence, however, and did and said nothing to invite renewed Soviet/Russian intervention. Finland maintained its independence and was able to focus on the prosperity and well-being of its people. The result is its perennial listing near the top of the world rankings for best country and citizen happiness.[12] Finland maintained this policy until 2023 when it joined NATO as a result of Russia's invasion of another of its neighbours, Ukraine, suggesting it had reached the limits of accommodation and its leaders decided to seek strength among like-minded states.

War is a contest between two adversaries, each intent on imposing their will on the other. Forcing your opponent to accept your will – to make your enemy do what you want it to do – is the objective of all wars. The acceptance by your enemy of your desires represents their agreement to what you are seeking in going to war. Typical reasons for starting a war include the acquisition of territory, control of or preferential access to a resource, the settlement of a point of pride or honour, or even the extinction of the target as an independent state. As each combatant may have allies, war can involve coalitions of states fighting towards the common goal of giving their common enemy or enemies no option but to concede the point of dispute. War continues until one side is reduced to such a physical and moral state that it believes itself incapable of continuing the struggle or until exhaustion forces both sides to postpone the settlement of the dispute until a later opportunity.[13] 'Loss of hope ... is what decides the issues of war,' according to Liddell Hart.[14]

When a war begins, one party is typically the aggressor, namely the side that starts it, and the other is the defender, the side that is the target of the aggression. There is of course a third option other than that of being an aggressor or defender. When a state is attacked its leaders may decide that the best course of action is not to fight – to surrender outright and accept the will of their enemy without resistance. This usually occurs when one side is so overmatched that any resistance would be futile, if not foolish, and there would be no dishonour in not resisting. When Germany invaded Denmark on 9 April 1940, the Danes knew they had neither a favourable geography, sufficient military strength, nor the prospect of allies coming to their timely aid, whereas the Germans possessed overwhelming force and a willingness to use it with extreme brutality. Any resistance by the Danes would have unnecessarily cost lives, and the government surrendered six hours after the Germans crossed the border. Further resistance would have had no effect on the outcome and the Danes rightly accepted their fate. The cost to Denmark was sixteen soldiers killed.

Those who conduct or study war divide its waging into a number of levels. Traditionally, there are just two: strategy and tactics. Carl von Clausewitz provides the classic definition of strategy. He calls it 'the use of engagement for the object of the war'.[15] By this he means the application and coordination of military power in such a manner as to achieve the goal of the war. Because strategy deals with the waging of war, military professionals often refer to it as military strategy or defence strategy, thereby distinguishing it from grand strategy, which will be discussed in the next chapter.

Tactics means the planning for and waging of battle, or in Clausewitz's words, 'the use of armed forces in the engagement'.[16] In the second half of the twentieth century, military practitioners added a third level – operations. It is understood to be the 'level at which campaigns and major operations are planned, sequenced and directed'.[17] The operational level became essential because since the First World War it has no longer been possible to decide a war between major powers in a single battle. Instead, it has become necessary to orchestrate a series of blows over an extended time period, to overcome a large modern state's reserve of resources. In a sense, the operational level is the linking level of war in which actions taken in all domains – land, sea, air, space and cyber – are coordinated and integrated to advance towards the strategic aim.

The state that starts a war must have a goal and its leaders must believe that employing violence is the best or perhaps only means by which they can achieve it. The victim of this aggression, if it decides to fight, has a goal too: to deny the attacker its objective. The defender, therefore, has the easier task, for it is harder to impose a new relationship between states than it is to maintain an existing one. The defence is about self-preservation and is 'driven by the imperative of not allowing the enemy to impose his will on us'.[18] For these reasons military thinkers accept that if all other elements are equal, the defensive form of war is naturally stronger than the offensive.[19]

However, no one wants to fight a war as equals. Instead, each side seeks to gain an advantage over their opponent by developing new technologies, upgrading existing weapons, conceiving of better ways to fight, increasing the size and efficiency of their forces, and improving the training of their troops, to name but a few techniques employed. The intent is to achieve a superiority over the enemy that enables your forces to press harder than the opponents are able to resist. Throughout the history of war, at different times the interaction of various factors favoured the offensive or the defensive, allowing one to have a dominant advantage over the other. In the First World War, the ability of the combatants to cover the approach to their positions with enormous firepower, coupled with the use of barbed wire and fortifications, allowed the defence to dominate and created the stalemate of the Western Front. Almost 2000 years earlier, the superior training and tactics of Roman soldiers and the efficiency of Rome's bureaucracy built a way of war in which the offensive dominated and resulted in the creation of an empire that endured for centuries.

In our own age, the combination of ubiquitous sensors with precision long-range strikes and uncrewed platforms (drones) has again shifted the pendulum of war to the side of the defence, giving it a natural superiority and thereby complicating the effort of the attacker. As I have written elsewhere, defenders today have the ability to create killing zones hundreds if not thousands of kilometres in depth over the approaches to their territory.[20] Sensors mounted in satellites, aircraft, on or below the ground and floating on the sea can reveal targets that emit any kind of signal across the magnetic, sound, and visual spectrums. Once identified, a target can be destroyed by precision missiles, armed drones or long-range artillery. If it can be seen or detected, it can be killed.

To achieve its goal, an aggressor needs to force an opponent to concede, but the defender's ability to hold and kill an enemy at a distance forestalls this. Therefore, today the defence enjoys the natural advantages that Clausewitz observed, compounded by the superior advantages that contemporary technology confers. Until the pendulum of war shifts again, through offensive innovation, the defender will continue to enjoy an advantage. Clausewitz reached his conclusion based on personal observation during the Napoleonic Wars. More recently, his insight has been confirmed through quantitative analysis. Historian Christoper A Lawrence in *War by the Numbers* was able to establish the natural superiority of the defence and the wisdom of the weak assuming a defensive posture.[21]

As the above suggests, being the defender is not a passive activity. This is because the defence exists in two parts: waiting and acting. The defender must wait because it is not up to it to start a war – that is what the aggressor does. This means that the military of a state that is satisfied with the status quo, such as Australia, should spend most of its existence in preparation and thinking on how best to defend itself while waiting for another power to threaten it with violence. Once the aggressor initiates the war, however, the defender is no longer obligated to be forbearing. Its forces need not simply endure the enemy's blows. Instead, the defender must respond with brutal violence of its own in order to convince the aggressor that its efforts are futile and its goal not worth the price it will have to pay. This means that the defender must be prepared to attack when the opportunity presents.[22] For the defender, as Clausewitz writes, 'a sudden powerful transition to the offensive – the flashing sword of vengeance – is the greatest moment'.[23]

Military thinkers combine the strategic and tactical levels of war with the roles of attacker and defender to define four forms of war.[24] They are:

1. Strategic Offensive
2. Strategic Defensive
3. Tactical Offensive
4. Tactical Defensive

Each opponent merges one of the strategic forms with one of the tactical forms, resulting in the following possibilities that a state will follow as it prosecutes a war:

- Strategic Offensive with the Tactical Offensive
- Strategic Offensive with the Tactical Defensive
- Strategic Defensive with the Tactical Offensive
- Strategic Defensive with the Tactical Defensive

The combination of the Strategic Offensive with the Tactical Defensive is best used when an aggressor intends to make limited gains. In this situation, the aggressor seizes its objective in a conflict's opening phase and challenges its victim to take it back. In such a situation of limited ambition, the aggressor is able to employ the natural strength of the defence to help secure its aim.[25] China's occupation and militarisation of contested islands in the South China Sea is an excellent example of the Strategic Offensive/Tactical Defensive combination at work, even if this did not take place in a war. It will prove far more difficult for other nations to dislodge the Chinese than it was for China to carry out the occupation.[26]

In the case of wars for more open-ended ambitions, the aggressor will resort to the Strategic Offensive in combination with the Tactical Offensive with the objective of defeating their opponent in battle. An aggressor that does not seek battle can only achieve defeat. By contrast, the defender is almost always limited to the Strategic Defensive, but can combine it with either of the two tactical forms. The most likely form, at least initially, is the Strategic Defensive with the Tactical Defensive. If successful, this combination will lead to the exhaustion and frustration of the attacker and result in the maintenance of the status quo, the Strategic Defensive's goal.

There have been cases where both combatants assumed the Strategic Offensive at the commencement of a war. In the Franco-Prussian War of 1870–71 both sides believed themselves to be on the Strategic Offensive. This is because Louis-Napoleon, France's Emperor, had miscalculated after having been adroitly manoeuvred into war by Prussia's Minister President, Otto von Bismarck. Prussia and its German allies were the ones that harboured offensive goals and France found out too late that its proper form of war was the Strategic Defensive. The result was France's defeat.

Conflicts that feature several distinct theatres may also result in the assumption of multiple forms of war. In the First World War, Germany faced a two-front war. In the Western Theatre it assumed the Strategic Offensive, hoping to drive France quickly out of the war so that it could shift troops to the Eastern Front against Russia. Initially, it aimed to fight a defensive war in the east. At the same time, the French and Russian armies also assumed the Strategic Offensive, similarly hoping to overwhelm Germany's armies in rapid campaigns.

A state does not have to maintain the same form of war for the entire conflict. At the onset of the Second World War in the Pacific, Japan was on the Strategic Offensive. Having seized the territory and resources it sought, it then transitioned to the Strategic Defensive. Conversely, the United States and its allies, including Australia, began the war as the defenders but as soon as it could America took to the Strategic Offensive and marched towards Tokyo with the goal of unconditional surrender and the remaking of Japanese society, a mission it accomplished.

For Australia, its present condition as a status quo state in combination with the availability and capabilities of modern weapons and sensors means that its natural and most powerful philosophy of war is the Strategic Defensive, in combination with the Tactical Defensive. All the factors that mandate the adoption of the Strategic Defensive are present.

- Australia is a status quo state with no interest in attacking anyone.
- If Australia was to go to war, its goal would be to preserve the world as it is, not to prey on other states.
- Australia is relatively weak militarily.
- Australia's geography favours the defence.
- Australia, if it chose, could acquire modern weapons and sensors with which it could hold an aggressor at bay a considerable distance from its own territory.

Australia's goal in such a war would be to make an opponent pay to such an extent that the latter lost interest in the war and agreed to a continuation of the antebellum relationship between the two sides.

It should be stressed that being on the Strategic Defensive does not mean Australia cannot or should not attack. Rather, the ADF must take every opportunity to inflict pain and loss of personnel and material on an opponent because it is essential to raise the price of war higher than what the aggressor is willing to pay. However, the aims of such attacks must always be defensive in scope because of Australia's war goal – the retention of the status quo.

Even though Australia is a natural Strategic Defensive state it has generally not acted or fought as one. In many of its wars, it has consistently rejected the form of war that best suits its nature. This is because Australia is a sub-imperial power. Australia's great power partners, first Britain and now the United States, have both been natural Strategic Offensive states, intent on building and securing their empires and forcing other states to do their will. Since its establishment Australia has participated in numerous wars, but in every case as a junior partner in a coalition led by its great power protector. In these wars, Australia's leaders have placed the nation's military forces under the mandate of the imperial power. The result is a contradiction: when Australia goes to war it generally does so as a Strategic Offensive state rather than its proper condition as a Strategic Defensive one. This is a serious contradiction because the result is a defence force optimised to contribute to its imperial power's wars and not to actually defend Australia.

Conclusion

Waging war is a serious business. So is its preparation. The first step is that a nation's leaders must be realistic about the kind of state they represent. This means they will need to be honest about their country's attributes and desires in relation to other countries. Australia's leaders have consistently avoided this honesty, instead automatically defaulting to their imperial partner's desires.

For much of its history, this did not matter because Australia belonged to the dominant empire. When challenged in the First and

Second World Wars and during the Cold War, Australia's imperial leader eventually prevailed. In none of these cases was victory easily obtained and the wars were long, hard fought and expensive. Perhaps, then, Australia's leaders can be forgiven for embracing the policy of dependence and accepting its consequences.

However, the situation is changing. The world is heading towards a more dangerous and violent future that may contain more state-on-state wars such as the current conflict in Ukraine, or see entire regions collapse into ungoverned spaces due to the stress of climate change. While the United States is still tremendously powerful, it is a troubled nation that some commentators fear is on the path to social collapse if not civil war.[27] A 2022 Economist/YouGov Poll reported that 40 per cent of Americans expect the nation to divide in two within the next ten years.[28] Survival compounds continue to proliferate, while it is estimated that twenty million Americans are preparing for cataclysm.[29] Despite the obsequious fealty of the nation's political class, American reliability as Australia's protector is undergoing a decline that may prove irreversible. Australia has also run out of options for the role of great power protector if the United States were to abandon the job.

Fortunately, our nation is not without options. Its geography, wealth, educated population and the defensive advantage of modern weapons allow it to explore alternatives to continuing as a sub-imperial partner. All the factors that mandate the posture of a Strategic Defensive state are in Australia's favour. The next two chapters explore how Australia becomes one.

4

LAYING THE FOUNDATION FOR THE STRATEGIC DEFENSIVE

HAVING ESTABLISHED THAT THE philosophy of the Strategic Defensive is the most suitable defence posture for Australia, the next step is to outline the requirements for its achievement. Its implementation will require more than just a redefinition of how the ADF will organise and fight. Like all successful government policy, the Strategic Defensive must be built on a sound foundation of appropriate funding, well-thought-out planning, a deep appreciation of and reflection upon the requirements, and a willingness to adapt and embrace new opportunities, as well as the ability to abandon what is no longer useful. Lastly, the Strategic Defensive, as is the case for all defence policy, needs guidance from the highest level of government planning through the creation of a grand strategy. This would be the nation's first grand strategy, the lack of which up to now is an oversight that has undermined the efficacy of all previous defence policies. Unfortunately, the government rarely advances beyond the superficial in all these requirements because by following a policy of dependency it does not have to treat defence with the seriousness it requires. This chapter will outline the steps needed to create the requisite foundation that will enable the Strategic Defensive to replace dependency as Australia's defence philosophy.

The money imperative

Security costs money and there is no easy way around this fact. If citizens want to be secure from potential threats, they have to accept the need to provide the government with the necessary funds to support a military force and other forms of security apparatus. If government leaders are to fulfil the obligation of providing security to their people, they must be willing to expend money on the citizenry's behalf to create the defence capability the nation requires. In doing this they must make the case to the public as to why these funds are needed and to what end. Moreover, politicians must spend this money wisely, because once consumed it cannot be used for anything else.

Money is a finite resource and its expenditure comes with opportunity costs – those things the public may also want but for which there are no longer funds available. Therefore, political leaders must be focused on military capabilities that meet the national need and fund only those that provide the effect sought – itself an objective that requires much thought and precise definition – and at the best price. A capability is more than just a tank or plane. Capabilities are made up of all the inputs – trained personnel, equipment, support and maintenance – needed for it to work effectively within a nation's military philosophy. Often, there may be more than one way to achieve a given effect. For example, if the government wants the ADF to be capable of hitting a hostile target with a missile, this can be achieved by numerous means – firing from a ship, dropping by a plane or launching from a land-based platform – and each comes at a different cost and with different personnel and training requirements, targeting protocols and support systems. The selected platform should be the one that performs the required task in the needed time frame and at the lowest price.

For fiscal year 2023–4, the most recent year for which figures were available at the time of writing, the Australian government provided the Department of Defence with a budget of $52.55 billion, which includes the Australian Signals Directorate's (ASD) allocation of $2.47 billion.[1] According to budget analyst Marcus Hellyer, this represents an increase of 7 per cent on the previous year, but when predicted inflation is taken into account, the additional funding is in the order of a more modest 3 per cent. This would be a good outcome compared to the previous year when inflation, Hellyer notes, effectively wiped out any budget growth.[2] As will be explained below, the government tipped additional monies into the defence account as a result of AUKUS and the 2024 *Integrated Investment Program*.

While $52.55 billion makes a good headline, it is not the full story and should not be the focus of anything more than fleeting attention. What really matters is whether or not the budget provided is able to meet what the government says it intends to do, and if what the government plans to do represents a sensible and wise commitment of the public purse. Additionally, it is important that the government go the next step and actually allocate monies to the budget that meet the expenditure required. Underfunded commitments make a good announcement, but they add nothing to capability and only push the date of financial reckoning into the future. For example, a series of governments undermined the *2009 Defence White Paper* by allowing a mismatch to exist between the document's strategic assessment and their own willingness to meet the cost. From these perspectives, there are a number of pressing concerns with the current budget.[3]

According to Max Blenkin of the *Australian Defence Magazine*, the 2023–4 defence budget lacks detail on what it expects the nuclear-powered submarines will cost over the next four years, the excuse for the omission being commercial sensitivities. This is the same rationale given for the absence of a costing for the government's purchase of a stake in the radar company CEA.[4] An analysis prepared by the Parliamentary Library admits that the 2023 *DSR* was 'light on detail about the money needed to fulfil the Government's vision'.[5] The lack of information for the public's interrogation is a chronic problem for the defence budget and leads to a knowledge gap which allows the government to avoid having to justify capability expenditure. For example, to meet the initial requirements of the AUKUS agreement the government has tipped an additional $30 billion into defence coffers with a large share of this money being donated to American and British corporations to improve their submarine-building infrastructure.[6] Why Australian taxpayers are supporting foreign corporations is not really explained. To date there has not been much progress in nailing down the cost of the nuclear-powered submarines, which is estimated to be about $368 billion. All that is clear is that the government's three recent major defence initiatives – AUKUS, the *DSR* and the enhanced surface fleet – will require huge sums of additional monies that will need to be found from the public purse.[7]

The mechanism with which Defence manages its capability acquisition program is known as the *Integrated Investment Program* (*IIP*). The *IIP* guides the purchase of capability over a multi-year rolling window. Items that appear on the *IIP* have been authorised by the government. However, there is no guarantee that these purchases will actually occur. After the Albanese government took office, it discovered that the previous government had made numerous announcements of equipment acquisitions but neglected to allocate the necessary funds. In effect, these were hollow acquisitions whose funding had been put off to the future. The *DSR*'s authors discovered that over the decade to 2032–3 there was $42 billion in additional Defence spending without the provision of any commitment of funds in the Commonwealth budget. The much-hyped ASD Redspice program was short by $7.9 billion and the critical Guided Weapons and Explosive Ordnance Enterprise needed $32.2 billion. Overall, a fourth of what Defence planned to buy had no funds allocated for the purchase.[8]

Such budget shenanigans are not the only problem for defence finances. Hellyer objects to what he calls a 'business as usual' approach to the defence budget. He points out that there is a disconnect between the government's language, which is one of urgency regarding the threat, and the lack of any sense of haste reflected in the budget. After all, Albanese has said the nation 'confronts the most challenging strategic circumstances since the Second World War'.[9] Hellyer writes:

> The heart of the problem in the 2023–24 Defence budget is a failure to start at the beginning: from a thesis setting out the defence force the country ideally needs to meet its strategic circumstances, then confronting it with an antithesis – the amount of money the government would prefer to spend on defence, and then synthesising these into an affordable but effective force structure somewhere in between.[10]

The Australian Strategic Policy Institute also perceives a disconnect between strategic direction and the defence budget, but takes comfort in what it claims to be 'all indications point[ing] to a steady and possibly substantial rise'.[11]

One of the recommendations of the *DSR* was that Defence rebuild and reprioritise the entire *IIP*. Marles released the 2024 *IIP* on 17 March, along with the *National Defence Strategy* (*NDS*). The new *IIP* outlines the funds required over the coming decade, but in doing so manages to repeat some of the deficiencies that undermined the previous government's *IIP*. It conveniently overlooks financial pressures that will prove its undoing. It ignores the past three years of high inflation, and the prospect of future inflation, and its effect on Defence's purchasing power. According to Hellyer, Defence would need another $40 billion over the 2024 *IIP* to offset inflation. Hellyer also notes that most of the new money provided is for the SSN enterprise. This means that the overall pot of money has not grown by much and the government will still need to find funding for the other planned capability programs.[12] Another point of concern is that the *IIP* provides only an additional $5.7 billion over the forward estimates (the next four years) while backloading the rest – $50.3 billion – to the decade's second half.[13] The spending goalposts shift again into the future, pushing off the required hard decisions to someone else's watch. The astute reader will note that two elections will pass before Defence starts to receive significant increases in money. Perhaps worse than this, the *IIP* achieves its funding by cancelling projects whose value had already been proven.

The maritime domain share of the budget, at 38 per cent, is more than the other domains combined (land – 15 per cent, air – 14 per cent and cyber – 7 per cent), with the nuclear-powered submarines and Hunter-class frigates absorbing nearly all of it. This means the majority of the new capability money will be spent on warships whose introduction to service is a decade or more distant.[14] Essentially, Australia is prioritising a future capability desire over present needs as it again commits to vessels for which it has yet to provide a justification. As Allan Gyngell has noted, all that the government provides the public is a sales patter that 'China is more assertive, rules-based order under threat, nuclear submarines are just what Australia needs ... but nothing about the why'.[15]

Part of the *IIP*'s funding magic is what it no longer includes. While the maritime domain is the priority, two of its previously approved programs are no more. Both of the planned Joint Support Ships have been deleted, along with the mine countermeasure and hydrographic vessels. Logistics is a part of war that the ADF underappreciates, so it is perhaps not surprising that the support ships have been cut. Unfortunately, this occurs at the same time as the Army is being told to become a littoral force, which will require it to manoeuvre over water across the region. These ships would probably have come in handy to provide soldiers with the support they would need. One of the wins in the *IIP* is the investment in nautical mines, which the ADF can use to close maritime choke points and protect harbours. This makes the cutting of mine countermeasure ships all the more questionable because it is these ships that are used to remove mines. Presumably, the enemy also has mines and may seek to restrict the RAN's ability to manoeuvre. There is little doubt that these small ships will be missed, precisely when they are needed most.[16] The other capability that is underfunded is autonomous uncrewed systems (drones), which received only a token allocation, thereby assuring that the ADF remains far behind other countries in this new addition to the art of war. Defence's singular initiative in this area was in November 2024 with the release of a tender seeking a partner to undertake market analysis. As the war in Ukraine demonstrates, other militaries are well beyond such a preliminary step. Known as Land 156, Defence's counter-drone program serves to underscore just how far behind the ADF lags in the fielding of these weapons and the lack of urgency with which the government pursues new acquisition and capability development.[17]

While there are many problems with the government's expenditure plan for the ADF, even without them it would still be wasteful because it will do little to improve the nation's security – as will be highlighted in depth in the next chapter – while ignoring better options for the nation's security. The Strategic Defensive will also require the expenditure of funds, but the difference is that its adoption offers a security policy that meets the nation's natural condition as a status quo state. The government's reluctance to provide detail on its plans to the nation's citizens suggests that our leaders may not be able to justify what they have initiated, other than it being similar to what was done in the past. The likely result of the current acquisition trajectory remains an ADF that is best suited for supporting the United States, not defending Australia, a waste of public funds, and a public that has been dudded – again.

The need to change – sensibly

One of the eternal features of war is the desire by combatants to gain an advantage over their enemies. No military seeks, or should seek, to fight as equals. The first known such competition took place in the fourth millennium BC when a metal worker, whose name is lost to time, figured out how to cast a copper mace. The superiority of the copper version over existing stone ones was evident in battle. In response, other peoples adapted and made copper maces of their own or invested in a range of weapons such as metal pointed spears and arrows, along with protective armour and helmets.[18] It should be noted that the search for military advantage is not limited to the field of technology. The success of the Roman Empire, for example, was not so much a result of better weapons but came about thanks to the creation of a superior combat system, the intensive training that filled a legionnaire's day and the existence of a bureaucracy that provided the legions with weapons and supplies.[19]

When two combatants fight in the same manner it is known as waging symmetrical warfare, while to fight differently is called asymmetrical warfare. In the eighteenth century, soldiers stood arrayed in several lines, shoulder-to-shoulder, firing their muskets at their similarly armed and arranged opponents. Both sides waged battle symmetrically. By contrast, the Vietnam War provides an example of an asymmetrically waged war. The United States brought to the war superior technology, massive firepower and seemingly limitless resources, with which they sought to annihilate their enemy. The North Vietnamese and their Viet Cong partners knew they could not match US strength, so they correctly refused to fight the way the Americans wanted. Instead, they applied the ideas of Mao Tse-Tung and the lessons of the communist victory in China, and, by pursuing guerrilla-style warfare, largely negated US advantages. They avoided battle except at times and places of their own choosing, and played a waiting game of strategic exhaustion, which they eventually won.[20]

I am not recommending that the ADF should fight its next war as guerrillas, unless the particular circumstances of a future conflict suggest such an approach is Australia's best option. What is critical is that Australia should not plan to fight a symmetrical war, particularly against a stronger opponent. Unfortunately, by investing in a force that aligns with America's philosophy of war – the Strategic Offensive – it is building an ADF that is not optimised for defence, while creating a force that will be unable to respond effectively to conflicts triggered by climate change. Instead of looking at a different way to think about how to fight, such as the Strategic Defensive, the ADF is preparing to fight China as equals.

The government's ADF modernisation program, as mandated by AUKUS and described in recent defence policy documents, is about taking the existing organisation and design and making it larger and more modern but not more fit for purpose to defend the nation in the emerging security environment. Despite the government's claims that it is taking a fundamentally new approach to defence, it is really offering more of the same, with the main difference being one of terminology not content. Thus, instead of a 'balanced force' the ADF is to become a 'focused force' that is to be optimised for 'impactful projection' – whatever that might be.[21] The *National Defence Strategy* gives climate change passing reference but provides no substance on what Defence plans to do or what it considers should be the ADF's role.[22] The surface ships that the government has announced are neither novel solutions to the challenges Australia faces nor materially different from those already in service around the world, the only distinguishing difference being their greater price tag for less capability. The RAAF is in a similar position in that its primary strike platforms are piloted aircraft that are comparable to those fielded by other air forces. Furthermore, the government has stressed the need for greater interoperability with the military of the United States, tying the ADF to the American way of war for the foreseeable future. The *NDS* calls the alliance with the United States 'fundamental to our national security' and aims for even deeper defence engagement.[23] It appears that Australia, although a relatively weak power, is preparing to participate in a symmetrical war, under a US umbrella, rather than one that features the different opportunities of an asymmetric one and which prioritises the nation's defence. In step with the US military, Australia is building a future force that wants to fight a potential adversary, such as the Chinese, as equals. Yet Australia and China are not equals – Australia is the weaker and cannot win a symmetrical fight. Therefore, the government should focus its future acquisition program on exploiting asymmetric ways of war.

Besides its great cost and the abrogation of sovereignty, Australia also missed a potentially useful opportunity in its commitment to AUKUS. Had the government sought alternative approaches to security it would have seen benefit in pushing for a third pillar, an asymmetric-focused one. The Chinese have shown themselves to be masters of competition below the threshold of war, as have the Russians, but those designing AUKUS decided not to include in its ambitions the recent lessons on the accomplishments by soft power and 'grey zone' activities in shaping the conflict environment and causing multiple headaches and confusion for a potential adversary. Andrew Bacevich explains the reason for this oversight. The preferred response by the United States to problems is usually a military one in which missiles fly, bombs drop and enemies die. In recent decades the United States has acted with a 'heedless absence of self-restraint, with shallow moralistic impulses overriding thoughtful strategic analysis'.[24] But this need not have been the case. For the

United States – and through its dependency, Australia – war should not be the only way to manage global events.[25]

There is still time for the AUKUS agreement to include a Pillar III that promotes the understanding of the political dynamic, develops soft power capability that links to objectives, coordinates 'grey zone' activities across the allies, and infuses knowledge and awareness of potential adversaries into all operations. The goal of such efforts would be to weaken or confuse a potential adversary to the point that conflict does not become necessary to achieve one's goals. The Chinese understand this and they practise it. As Sun Tsu observes, 'to subdue the enemy without fighting is the acme of skill'.[26] AUKUS can and should be an opportunity to prioritise the acquisition of the requisite skills.

There are numerous liabilities in the government's future plan for the ADF and all derive from a reluctance to embrace change on the intellectual level. At great expense the ADF will acquire a host of new and updated platforms, with the RAN taking the largest share of the budget. Yet the operational design of the resulting force, with a few exceptions such as the Army's acquisition of land-based missiles, will be minimally different from the existing one and its way of conducting war. This is a failure of imagination and intellect, and shows a reluctance to move outside of existing comfort zones that any disruptive thinking would require. Amazingly, despite their clear relevance, autonomous uncrewed systems are an afterthought in the *IIP*. In part, this lack of imagination is a function of the government's insistence on deepening the ADF's interconnection with the US military, an insistence that closes off other possibilities from consideration.

Lastly, and ultimately, the Australian government's longstanding refusal to countenance the development of anything that aspires to the level of grand strategy, as the next section will explain, keeps the ADF from exploring new ideas and inhibits the search for better solutions. All of Australia's defence policy papers that underpin the current build-up have been written without any grand strategic-level guidance from the government. This means that the Australian government is spending lots of money, without first deciding what they want the ADF to do and in the absence of an overarching philosophy such as the Strategic Defensive for guidance.[27]

The need for a grand strategy

Defining and implementing a grand strategy is the most critical factor in assuring a nation's future security. It is the master plan by which a state achieves its policy goal or goals in the security realm. The new *NDS* does not aspire to this level of future planning because its focus is on security as appreciated by the Department of Defence – that is, how the ADF can provide for the nation's security. This is only justifiable due to Australia's very narrow understanding of what national security actually is. In effect, the *NDS* is a *military* strategy, perhaps unsurprisingly since its authorship is the Department of Defence.

Grand strategy involves more than just military power and is different from military strategy. Rather, 'grand strategy considers all the resources at the disposal of the nation (not just military ones), and it attempts to array them effectively to achieve security in both peace and war'.[28] Thus, grand strategy is a whole-of-government activity and its stakeholders are not limited to a Department of Defence. Every nation's diplomatic, economic, demographic, environmental, cultural and social representatives have inputs into the development of grand strategy, as well as the making of the policy to achieve it.[29]

The concept of grand strategy has many definitions and its interpretation has not stood still. Scholar of military affairs Edward Mead Earle included what has become a much-cited definition for grand strategy in his classic 1943 work, *Makers of Modern Strategy*. He calls it 'that which so integrates the policies and armaments of the nation that the resort to war is either rendered unnecessary or is undertaken with the maximum chance of victory'.[30] A more recent, and briefer, definition is provided by two historians of war, Ian Speller and Christopher Tuck, who call grand strategy 'the application of national resources to achieve national/alliance policy objectives'.[31]

Seeking to highlight the character of grand strategy, historian Williamson Murray takes a different approach. He emphasises the need for policy-makers to accept that grand strategy exists in a world of flux, and constant change and adaptation are its companions.[32] He likens it to how French peasant soup is made: 'a mixture of items thrown into the pot over the course of a week and then eaten, for which no recipe can possibly exist'.[33] While there may not be a recipe for the making of grand strategy, there are certain rules. Murray points out that to achieve a useful grand strategy requires an acceptance that the future is unforeseeable. Consequently, the only guide for those thinking about grand strategy is the past, for which they must have a deep understanding, and the present, which requires a comprehensive and realistic appreciation. The other requirement is that one must possess deep knowledge and a clear-eyed assessment of one's opponents and also of oneself. Making useful grand strategy does not suffer fools.[34]

Grand strategy is a requirement for both war and peace. In fact, it is even more important to have a grand strategy in peacetime because it allows a state to respond to a problem with something other than violence – a grand strategy incorporates other levers of power than the military, whose sole function is to apply force, or its threat. Competition between states is more common than readers might realise. The normal relationship between rival states is one of competition as they vie with each other across all elements of human endeavour in order to advance or protect their interests. Sometimes this competition may solely be about prestige, such as the race to the moon or which country wins the most medals at the Olympics, but it never truly goes away. As a sub-imperial power, Australia cannot avoid being drawn into the contest between the great powers and consequently the perception of rivalry with China. Thus, the necessity for a grand strategy remains.

For a state, grand strategy's most important role is that it sets a destination. It is the future objective for which a nation's political leaders will develop plans and implement policies so that the country can pursue the optimal route to where it wants to go. An example might help explain the aspirational nature of the possession of a grand strategy. One of the more serious risks Australians accept every day, even if most of them do not know it, is the country's near total reliance on imported petroleum liquid fuels. More than half of Australia's imported refined fuels come from South Korea and Singapore, with significant quantities sourced from Malaysia, Japan and Taiwan, all brought here on shipping routes that could be easily disrupted by China if it wanted to do so. In fact, according to a 2022 analysis, 90 per cent of Australia's refined fuel imports are vulnerable to interdiction in the South and East China seas. Interestingly, in 2022 China itself provided 4.11 per cent of Australia's refined fuel.[35]

Without a steady supply of liquid fuels, much of the Australian economy would quickly grind to a halt, supermarkets would soon empty of food, and employees would be unable to get to their places of work. Dependent on imported fuel, the ADF would no longer be able to operate. All this would occur within a few weeks since Australia maintains such small stocks of fuel in the country. If the nation's political leaders decided to reduce this weakness, one option could be to set a goal to replace the energy provided by liquid fuels with electricity generated from renewables. Engineer and inventor Saul Griffith outlines such a program of national electrification in his book *The Big Switch*.[36] It is a visionary objective worthy of a nation's grand strategic quest.

While aware of the dangers posed by the nation's dependence on imported liquid fuels, the government has taken only modest steps towards implementing a solution and, consequently, the risk remains. Measures implemented so far have included gaining access to the US Strategic Petroleum Reserve, a supply that is inconveniently located in the US state of Texas. Theoretically, the US government would allow Australia to draw upon its reserve in a global emergency, although the US consumer might have different ideas on permitting such a thing, as presumably the same disruption would be affecting Americans too. Even if the United States did release sufficient fuel, it would then have to get here, which would involve a voyage of about three weeks from loading, undertaken by tankers that Australia does not own or control. As a study from The Australia Institute drily points out, this is 'a crude policy fix'.[37] The government has also subsidised the building of some fuel tanks to increase storage, imposed a minimum stockholding obligation on fuel importers, and provided payments to upgrade Australia's two remaining refineries.[38]

Australia makes up for its lack of a grand strategy by doing what if often does – turning to its great power partner. Australia's preference is to simply adopt the position of its imperial leader. The nation's political class have never seen the need to adopt a grand strategy of our own. It is this history of filial attachment to the designs of Australia's great partners that has constrained the capacity and willingness of our leaders to think for themselves.[39]

The question then becomes what is the destination our political leaders have decided upon in making their decision to increase Australia's dependence on the United States? What vision for the future of the nation is achieved by the acquisition of nuclear-powered submarines, the investment in advanced military technologies under Pillar II and in increasing the nation's integration with and reliance on the United States? So far, if such a vision actually exists, the government has not decided to reveal it to the public. I suspect that no one responsible for making these decisions has thought that far. Another commentator on this subject has written:

> Put simply, there is no strategy behind the process [AUKUS]. There are plans, but nothing which takes into account the broader global strategic framework which will govern the threat and opportunity context which will apply to Australia and her alliance partners in the 70-year+ timeframe for the program. Neither is the program being considered in light of the imbalance it must, inevitably, bring to the Australian defence budget.[40]

The weakness in relying on an imperial leader – a foreign state, let us not forget – to define one's grand strategy is the risk that the senior partner may settle upon a poor or inappropriate one, or even go without. The United States has a mixed history of success at forging useful and implementable grand strategies. In the American Civil War, President Abraham Lincoln proved highly adept at the highest levels of war and set the parameters that would bring the Union victory.[41] Similarly, throughout the Second World War, Franklin D Roosevelt made all the major strategic decisions and did not hesitate to overrule his military commanders.[42] Throughout the Cold War, the United States was guided by a series of presidents who understood the perils as well as the opportunities in the competition with the Soviet Union.

Unfortunately, more recent administrations have not demonstrated a similar degree of grand strategic nous. George W Bush's failure to set an achievable grand strategy for his wars in the Middle East is largely responsible for the disasters that ensued there, while Donald Trump believed that the 'cost of global leadership was a losing proposition for America'.[43] Australia has hitched its strategic wagon to an imperial partner that in recent times has shown a significant lack of strategic judgement. America's deficiency in strategic thinking may prove to be a short-lived aberration. In coming years greater wisdom may prevail, or it may not, but the main point is that Australia will not have a say either way.

I do not want to suggest that deciding upon and implementing a grand strategy is easy – the reality is that it is an extremely difficult and complex task and potential adversaries will strive to undermine and counter any efforts on this front.[44] Yet without a grand strategy, a state lacks the ability to lay out a pathway to a secure place in the world. The future is not preordained and there are many paths that a state may take. Having an idea of the destination will make the task of providing Australia with the security it needs that much easier. Australia should, therefore, not be satisfied with simply accepting what the imperial partner provides in terms of strategic vision. The nation's leaders should take a firmer hand in shaping its destiny. Security strategist Gregory Copley captured the essence of the problem when he observed, 'Australia is, in many respects, at a pivotal point in its history, but seems not to have grasped this reality'.[45]

Conclusion

As a long-serving member of the Defence bureaucracy, I was in a position to observe the decision-making process for the acquisition of new capability even if I was not a participant in it. The process was a long, torturous path along which successive rotations of military personnel shepherded projects through a number of milestones, eventually reaching the point where the government decided to acquire something. Years passed slowly for those charged with this task. Throughout the process, the more astute realised that they could never answer one key question – what was the objective for which they had dedicated years of their careers? Government was always very interested in the cost of an acquisition and what percentage of the item could be made or assembled here, thereby generating jobs for Australian workers and a useful announceable for the politician. What strategic requirement the acquisition addressed was not on the political leadership's mind, although it was their responsibility to articulate the 'why'.

When prosecuting the art of war, Australia relies upon its great power protector for many things. Unfortunately, it also relies upon its protector for inappropriate things, such as a workable grand strategy and a vision for the future. The 2023 *DSR* makes a good case that there is now an appropriate sense of urgency surrounding Australia's security. Yet the government has not laid the foundation for successfully meeting a worsening security environment. The government has announced numerous acquisitions, but the amount of money needed remains unknown, while instead of being willing to embrace new ideas Australia's political leaders prefer the continuation of the existing trajectory. There is no indication that the government will consider the development of a grand strategy, the concept upon which security hangs. The inability to consider other options, including adopting a philosophy of war such as the Strategic Defensive, sees the nation locked into dependency with its sovereignty compromised and our future in the hands of a transactional US leadership that lacks a moral code and a sense of loyalty. Even worse, Trump shows no hesitancy in humiliating American friends and allies, as he did to the President of Ukraine during his visit to the White House in March 2025 and to all Canadians when he threatens to annex their country. Through all this, the more serious security threat of climate change remains unconsidered. The next chapter will drill deeply into what is wrong with the present defence policy, explore the utility of the Strategic Defensive and in doing so outline a better option whereby the nation can prepare for a more tumultuous age.

5

WHAT NEEDS TO BE DONE

THE *NATIONAL DEFENCE STRATEGY* (*NDS*) 2024 is the ADF's blueprint for the future. It requires the ADF to be able to:

1 **defend** Australia and our immediate region;
2 **deter** through denial any adversary's attempt to project power against Australia through our northern approaches;
3 **protect** Australia's economic connection to our region and our world;
4 **contribute** with our partners to the collective security of the Indo-Pacific; and
5 **contribute** with our partners to the maintenance of the global rules-based order.[1]

These are the same tasks given to the ADF in the 2023 *DSR* – an exact quote, including the bold type.[2]

The *NDS* shares the *DSR*'s belief that Australia's present strategic circumstances are now radically different, principally due to the 'intense China–United States competition [that] is the defining feature of our region and our time'.[3] The only difference being that with the passing of twelve months Australia's strategic environment has deteriorated further. Building on the *DSR*, the *NDS* concludes that the 'optimism at the end of the Cold War has been replaced by the uncertainty and tensions of entrenched and increasing strategic competition between the US and China'.[4] The *NDS* is a follow-on document from the *DSR* and incorporates within its pages the ambitions of the AUKUS agreement, the recommendations of the *Enhanced Lethality Surface Combatant Fleet* report and the objectives of the 2024 *Integrated Investment Program*.

It must be noted that there is nothing extraordinary in the five tasks identified above – they are remarkably similar to those contained in the *2016 Defence White Paper*, which also envisaged a rapid change in Australia's security environment. Eight years ago, unsurprisingly, the most important factor in driving what was seen as a worsening Australian security environment was the shifting of the balance of power between the United States and China.[5] In fact, I made the same observation even earlier in a 2012 paper, so the *NDS*'s assessment regarding the threat from China is not exactly revolutionary and serves to highlight the sluggishness of the government's reaction and the continuity in its policy.[6]

To build the future ADF, the *NDS* directs its leaders to provide the government with six capability effects, namely to:

1 project force;
2 hold a potential adversary's forces at risk;
3 protect ADF forces and supporting critical infrastructure in Australia;
4 sustain protracted combat operations;
5 maintain persistent situational awareness in our primary area of military interest; and
6 achieve decision advantage.[7]

The provision of six effects is a big ask for any military organisation, especially one with the size and resources of the ADF. The demand is even more challenging when several of the tasks are in conflict with one another and the government has elected not to provide any sense of priority. Hence, the government expects the ADF to be simultaneously able to protect the continent and project force overseas while holding an adversary at a distance and being ready to engage in close combat. Each of these tasks requires different equipment, training and doctrine and together would challenge a military that is much larger and more capable than the ADF. How this is to be resolved is left to the imagination of the Australian public.

The *NDS* is a rather staid document and is more notable for its continuities than for its radicalism, as are the means it identifies for the ADF to achieve its tasks. The solution it postulates to the threat from China is to acquire more things that are for the most part an update of existing ones, while demanding further integration with the US military as the standard to which the ADF should aspire. On the alliance, the *NDS* echoes the *DSR*'s conclusion that Australia's relationship with the United States must become even more fundamental to the nation's security.[8] The government has committed to building an ADF that is not fit for purpose, hopelessly enmeshed within US ambitions and not relevant for a state whose military philosophy is best suited for the Strategic Defensive.

Like their predecessors, the *NDS* and the *IIP* continue the Defence practice of employing vague language and avoiding specifics to justify the future ADF. The *NDS*'s new phrase *du jour* is 'impactful projection', but what this means is not defined. The provision of clarity is not essential because the unstated goal of both documents is for Australia to continue to position itself as a sub-imperial nation relative to its great power leader. Lastly, neither document makes any recommendations on how to address the other pressing national security threat – climate change – or identify the capabilities that the ADF will need to mitigate its dangers.

At the end of 2024, Defence released another policy document, the *Naval Shipbuilding and Sustainment Plan.* This document reiterated the principles and objectives of the previous plans and added nothing new to the understanding of the government's intention.[9]

Perhaps the most dangerous element of both the *DSR* and the *NDS* is the stress they place on deterrence. Deterrence is a problematic theory that relies heavily on the credibility of your determination, the certainty that you can inflict unacceptable cost on your opponent and the success of the messaging you send your adversary. In the case of China, Australia's policy of deterrence lacks intellectual integrity. China has no desire or need to attack Australia, so from that perspective deterrence is irrelevant. If China is determined to attack Taiwan, deterrence is also likely to fail because Beijing's stake over the island is far more vital than that of Canberra's or Washington's.[10]

More practically, if one accepts deterrence theory then one of the mandatory requirements to meet is the possession of sufficient mass to awe an aggressor, which is something that the *IIP* fails to provide. The future ADF will remain a largely undergunned bespoke force of capabilities that are too small to impress any major competitor, and acquisitions are spread out over decades. More alarmingly, the *NDS* avoids offering any detail on how the ADF will wage war if or when deterrence fails. The reader might recall the quote by Vegetius provided in chapter 3. He did not say, 'therefore, he who desires peace, let him prepare to deter'. Rome understood that while being able to deter was nice, being able to fight was what mattered. If Vegetius seems too distant, perhaps the words of George Washington resonate more: 'to be prepared for war is one of the most effectual means of preserving peace'.[11]

What is clear from these policy documents, and from recent statements by Australia's political leadership, is that the determination to remain dependent on the United States for the nation's security continues to be the most important, if not the sole, defence objective. No matter the present situation in Washington, Australia seems intent on maintaining its traditional relationship with the United States in the likely vain hope that it can avoid the abrupt dismissal that Europe, Canada and other long-term US friends and allies have recently suffered. In international affairs, one can profit from the lessons of others or learn them the hard way.

The following pages will describe what is wrong with the government's defence policy and the key capabilities it plans to buy, and suggests what Australia actually needs if true security is to result in accordance with the principles of the Strategic Defensive. In doing so it offers Australia the opportunity to implement what is needed to become a sovereign nation without the humiliation of a unilateral abandonment. It will first examine the capability programs that the government has committed to acquire, then outline why once in service most of these capabilities will not be able to do what is intended. Each capability's failure to perform as claimed will be a consequence of either out-of-date thinking, a force exchange imbalance with enemy platforms, the absence of a rationale and explainable utility, or advances in technology that will make the capability too vulnerable to use.

This chapter will offer a different ADF, one that is based on the philosophy of the Strategic Defensive. It will take each service in turn, starting with the RAN, since that is where the majority of the expenditure lies and since it is also the service at most risk of failure. Finally, the chapter will examine several important aspects of Australia's defence policy that are not service specific. These include the integration of ADF capabilities, force protection, the future of the alliance with the United States and the potential for Australia to base its security on nuclear weapons.

The future Royal Australian Navy

As a result of ineffectual government policy, poor planning and inadequate funding over many years and governments, the RAN, not to put too fine a point on it, is a mess. The fleet is too small, underarmed, outclassed by the warships of likely adversaries, and its ships are in danger of retirement before they can be replaced. Ship availability has become a chronic issue because the RAN is unable to recruit or retain enough sailors. The inadequacy of reflection on needs will produce a future fleet that looks very similar to the present one. Finally, as with the other services, uncrewed platforms received scant consideration in a quest to stay within existing comfort zones.[12]

Amazingly, so consistent has the RAN's mismanagement been, as well as the government's lack of any sense of urgency regarding it, that the fleet will contract further and is expected to bottom out in 2026 with just seven surface warships, a situation that will remain until about 2033.[13] The RAN's submarine fleet of six Collins-class boats is old and wearing out because of the government's failure to provide for their timely replacement. The 2009 *Defence White Paper* called for twelve new submarines, but after a series of false starts the replacement for the present Collins-class boats remains years away.[14] Now there is no choice but for the Collins boats to undergo an expensive life-of-type extension if the nation is to have any submarines capable of going to sea at all, pending the arrival of the Virginia-class submarines being purchased – hopefully – from the United States. The RAN's situation is a result of years, even decades, of mismanagement by governments of both major political parties.[15]

As the authors of the *DSR* considered their recommendations, the best they could do for the navy was to advise the government to commission an independent review on the RAN's surface warship needs. The Albanese government turned to two retired vice-admirals – William Hilarides, USN, and Stuart Mayer, RAN – and a former Secretary of the Department of Finance, Rosemary Huxtable, to undertake the analysis. Delivered in February 2024 the *Enhanced Lethality Surface Combatant Fleet* (*ELSCF*) report managed to take a bad situation and make it worse.[16] The government accepted the authors' recommendations. It is worth going through each ship type in turn to highlight how, individually and in combination, the future surface RAN is an over-priced, poorly armed, technologically backward and strategically unnecessary contributor to the nation's security. One of the few things the report got correct was that if everything recommended is built, the result will be the largest surface fleet since the Second World War. Why this matters is not explained.

The RAN's most powerful warships are the existing Hobart-class air warfare destroyers, of which there are three. The *ELSCF* calls for the upgrade of their Aegis Combat System, an obvious and necessary step that will reduce the risk of their obsolescence. These ships will also see their ageing Harpoon anti-ship missiles replaced by the modern Naval Strike Missile, which has more than double the range. More questionably, the ships will also receive the Tomahawk land attack missile. These upgrades leave the ships' most important weapon system unchanged – the vertical launch system (VLS) for its missiles – which remain at forty-eight in number, far fewer than the number carried by similar sized warships of other navies. For surface warships the number of missiles they hold is the measure by which they are compared, and even when first designed these vessels had already fallen well short. Other navies know that if you cannot bring enough missiles to the fight, you should not be in it.

Amazingly, the much-troubled Hunter-class frigate program survived the *ELSCF* review despite being the subject of a scathing auditor-general's report in May 2023, as well as the Department of Defence's concession that the selection process was 'poorly executed' and the risks of choosing an 'immature design' inadequately appreciated.[17] The result of this is that the ships, at the time of writing, are already four years late and $15 billion over budget. The issues for these vessels are so obvious that numerous commentators at various points have recommended the Hunter's outright cancellation. Retired Admiral Rowan Moffat believes that these ships will never provide the RAN with a worthwhile capability. He calls these vessels, each with only thirty-two VLS, the most underarmed warship for their size in the world. Other concerns he has voiced are that the engine plant is underpowered for a ship of such tonnage and that its reliance on UK systems will greatly complicate the class's sustainment.[18] A former Chief of Navy, David Shackleton, also harbours major concerns regarding these ships and calls them 'seriously underarmed and underpowered for [their] size and therefore poorly suited to operations in our region'. He sees no sufficient reason to persevere with their construction.[19] In an earlier report written for the Australian Strategic Policy Institute, Shackleton was more direct: 'The Hunter program ... should be stopped'.[20]

A sense of the scale of the Hunter's underperformance in relation to similar warships operated by other nations is the 'cost per missile carried' comparison. As of 2022, the cost to place a missile on a Hunter frigate was A$158 million, whereas for the USN equivalent, the Arleigh Burke, the cost is only A$31 million.[21] Of course, the Hunter-class cost has blown out since 2022 so the actual divergence is likely to be even greater. Subject to a feasibility study, the Hunter frigates will be redesigned to accommodate the Tomahawk cruise missile, but the justification for these additions is unpersuasive.

Table 5.1 provides a comparison of the Hobart- and Hunter-class ships with warships of similar size built by other navies. As the table shows, other nations manage to build much more powerful ships at a much lower price. The cost does need to be viewed as indicative because of different national budget characteristics, currency exchange rates and the fact that some of the vessels were built some years ago. Still, the table suggests that Australian taxpayers will have to cover a substantial price premium to build inferior ships in Australia in order to maintain a sovereign ship-building industry. One wonders why this particular sovereign capability is considered so crucial, when the Australian government's underwriting of other industries that are arguably much more critical remains absent.

Table 5.1
Comparison of Hunter/Hobart ships with other nation builds

Nationality	Ship class	Began construction	Displacement in tons	Number of vertical missile launchers	Indicative cost per unit (USD)
Australia	Hunter	Future build	8700*	32	Estimated at $4.56 billion as of 2024
Australia	Hobart	2009	7700	48	$3 billion
United States	Arleigh Burke	1985	I – 8400 II – 8500 IIA – 9700 III – 9900	I – 90 II – 90 IIA – 96 III – 96	$2.2 billion
United States	Constellation	2022	7300	32	$1.05 billion
China	Type 055	2014	12 000	112	$888 million
Japan	Atago	2004	10 000	96	$1.48 billion
South Korea	Sejong	2007	10 600	128	$923 million

Weight is for a fully loaded vessel; Hunter class is still under design so final size and cost may change.
*The eventual displacement of the Hunter frigate is unclear as of this writing. A final displacement in excess of 10 000 tons is not unreasonable to assume.

To supplement the low firepower of the Hobart destroyers and the Hunter frigates the *ELSCF* has proposed a new class of warships – the Large Optionally Crewed Surface Vessel (LOCSV). The government explains the need for these vessels as enhancing 'the lethality and survivability of the joint integrated force'.[22] Why this will be the case is not clear since each vessel possesses just thirty-two vertical missile launchers. Even when sailing in combination with a Hobart frigate, the combined missile power is still considerably less than most vessels from any other nation's fleet. The LOCSV idea is reminiscent of what other navies have called an arsenal ship, but an undergunned one. The US Navy began to explore the arsenal ship concept in the 1990s as a means to apply massive firepower across the littoral environment. The number of missile cells the US Navy thought appropriate was in the order of 500.[23] While the United States never went ahead with the idea, the Republic of Korea Navy is planning to build three arsenal ships of their own design by the late 2020s, each carrying eighty missile cells.[24] Yet, in the age of the sea-strike missile, Australia sees thirty-two as an appropriate number. Since these vessels exist in name only, it is impossible to estimate the cost for the six the government is planning to build.

Being optionally crewed will also have the effect of massively increasing the cost of these vessels. By necessity each LOCSV will have an AI operating system as well as a crewed operating system. Adding sailors means increasing design complexity since the ship will require all the things humans need to survive at sea, such as fresh water, bunks, toilets and an adequately stocked galley, all of which adds weight, and results in a larger, more expensive ship. Moreover, each addition cascades through the ship's design. For example, if you increase a ship's weight you need bigger engines. Bigger engines necessitate larger fuel supplies, and on and on it goes. At the same time the AI operating system will require its own components to compensate for when a crew is not aboard. The result is a more complex vessel that is more expensive than it needed to be.

Fortunately, it is unlikely to matter because Australia will not have the capacity to start building the LOCSV until the late 2030s. Marles has announced that the LOCSV will be built in Western Australia at the Henderson shipyard, which is where the Offshore Patrol Vessels are currently under construction. Next in the queue are the Army's littoral manoeuvre vessels. Then, when these are delivered, the yard will build the general-purpose frigates that were called for in the *ELSCF* and which are described below. However, before the frigates start, Henderson will have to enlarge its building halls – the largest can manage ships up to 99 metres in length and the general-purpose frigates will be longer. According to Marles, Henderson will only start to build the LOCSV once the last frigate is in the water, which will not occur until sometime in the late 2030s or the 2040s. By the late 2030s, enemy ships will likely be carrying even more missiles than they do now – whereas the RAN is looking at taking possibly two decades to build a supplementary fires ship that will carry just thirty-two VLS. At some point, these vessels are likely to be quietly discarded, hopefully before not too much money is wasted.[25]

The rationale for this torpid build is the government's desire to assure a continuous ship build at the Henderson and Osborne (South Australia) shipyards. The driving force behind the RAN ship plan is not to defend the nation. Rather, it is industrial policy that will make sure both yards are kept busy, with the result that the RAN's build-up is decades-long and not optimised to meet the claimed urgent China threat. One can only conclude that the expansion of the surface fleet is not the priority the government claims.[26]

Meanwhile, the existing Anzac-class frigates continue to wear out due to their age and usage, and are becoming increasingly expensive to maintain. HMAS *Anzac* was decommissioned in May 2024 and *Arunta* will follow in 2026. The *ELSCF* recommended the rapid acquisition of a replacement, which it identifies as a general-purpose frigate. The desired vessels will be optimised for anti-submarine warfare, securing maritime trade routes and data cables, and escorting military assets. Because of their relatively small size they will likely carry only sixteen vertical missile launchers. Identifying them as Tier 2 vessels, in order to distinguish them from the more capable Hobart- and Hunter-class ships which are called Tier 1, the report urged the acquisition of at least seven and optimally eleven of these ships. So that they can join the fleet more quickly, the plan is to order an existing ship design, with the first three launched overseas before the transition is made to an Australian build. The government initially suggested four options: the Japanese Mogami, Germany's Meko A-200, South Korea's Daegu and Spain's ALFA3000.[27] By the end of 2024, the government had narrowed the contest down to either the Japanese or German vessel.[28]

The first new ships to join the fleet that are discussed in the *ELSCF* are the Offshore Patrol Vessels, which the government had ordered earlier as the replacement for the Armidale-class patrol boats and other minor vessels. Because they are lightly armed, their primary role will be constabulary missions. Construction of the initial two ships commenced in late 2018, and the first – the *Arafura* – was launched in 2023.[29] At the time of writing it was still undergoing sea trials. The authors of the *ELSCF* were not impressed by these vessels, describing them as an 'inefficient use of resources for civil maritime security operations' while also not possessing 'the survivability and self-defence systems to contribute to a surface combatant mission'. This is an assessment with which the Chief of Navy seems to agree. He has admitted that they are limited to a constabulary role because their 'survivability is very low so we'll keep her [the OPVs] out of the mix'.[30] It appears that the RAN has ordered warships that cannot fight and patrol vessels that are too inefficient to patrol. Nor do they have the capacity to clear mines or undertake maritime surveys. Consequently, the government agreed with the report's recommendation and reduced the original order from twelve to six – the steel for the sixth had already been cut. This is likely to prove six too many, especially since the projected total investment will near A$4 billion, an incredible sum for a ship that appears to lack utility.[31] The gap in patrol craft numbers will be met by the purchase of additional Evolved Cape-class patrol boats.

The more important question concerning the Offshore Patrol Vessels that the *ELSCF* authors left unanswered is whether it is appropriate for the RAN to be in the constabulary business in the first place. Traditionally, this has been a RAN mission because the government has had no other option. Since the raising of the Australian Border Force (ABF) this is no longer the case. The ABF is to receive a fleet of eleven Evolved Cape-class patrol boats (the RAN is to get eight, possibly fourteen, to compensate for the reduced number of Offshore Patrol Vessels). It is inefficient to have two fleets responsible for constabulary duties when one fleet can do the task. The RAN's primary role is warfighting, whereas the ABF, through its Maritime Border Command, has the authority to 'detect, deter, respond to and prevent civil maritime security threats'.[32]

Centralising border maritime security into a single organisation should be more efficient than having two with the same responsibility. For the RAN there is a benefit in transferring its patrol boats to the ABF. Doing so would free up scarce sailors for the crewing of more important vessels. Because the ABF will have less onerous terms of service and a lower training requirement than the RAN, it should be able to recruit maritime public servants more easily. The liability of an ownership transfer is that it would see the number of the navy's ship command positions reduce by fourteen, a development that mariners would find difficult to swallow when being in charge of a vessel is considered the high point of a career.

The *IIP* calls for the RAN to upgrade the missiles that its ships will carry. The RAN's existing fleet and new builds will receive the Naval Strike Missile, which has a range of 250 kilometres, and the Standard Missile (SM)-6, which can strike targets out to 200 kilometres. This is a big improvement over the venerable Harpoon that presently arms the fleet and only has a range of 120 kilometres. Unfortunately, Chinese ships carry anti-ship missiles with greater range and in larger numbers. China's YJ-18 anti-ship missile has a range of 470 kilometres, and the range of the YJ-21 is an impressive 1500 kilometres. Not only will the RAN be outgunned, it will also be outranged. In order to hit a Chinese ship, an Australian vessel must sail within the strike range of its adversary, meaning that an RAN warship must hazard its own sinking before it can fire at the enemy.

If the solution to fixing the RAN surface fleet is the unpromising acquisition of over-priced and undergunned ships, the prognosis for the subsurface fleet is not much better. Through the AUKUS deal, the RAN will receive three to five used USN Virginia-class submarines in the 2030s, followed by the building of the AUKUS-designed and -built boats in the 2040s. It is true that the Virginia boats are awesome warships. They are lethal, silent killers whose nuclear-powered operation provides great range, speed and endurance, allowing them to sail into distant waters and remain on station longer than is possible for a conventionally powered submarine. One can understand why the US Navy aims for a fleet of sixty-six Virginias. However, the requirements of the United States are not the same as those of Australia.

Buying these expensive vessels relies on several elements falling into place for which there are no guarantees and many possible points of failure. First, Australia must learn how to operate and maintain these vessels. Australia has no experience in sailing a nuclear-powered warship and lacks a domestic nuclear industry from which to source program management and maintenance skills. It is a big ask to expect the RAN to be able to step up and operate these vessels, particularly to the standard of the United States. Sending sailors to US and UK schools is a start, but a poor substitute for decades of experience and an existing nuclear culture. As one commentator notes, Australia 'should have considered SSNs decades ago'.[33]

Second, Australia is betting that the US submarine industry can solve its intractable production and maintenance delays. The USN needs to launch two submarines per year to meet its own fleet needs. To be able to sell Australia its three to five promised used Virginias, without affecting the operational availability of its fleet, the USN needs to launch 2.33 per year. Over the last decade, however, the US has averaged just 1.3 launches per year. Because of the inability to meet its own production targets, the 2025 Presidential Defence Budget requested money for just one new Virginia boat –

there was no yard capacity for more. The reduced production request sparked a reaction from the US Congress. Over 100 lawmakers signed a letter requesting the restoration of the second build. The Congressional Research Service went so far as to write another report on the AUKUS submarine project. Its authors again reviewed the liabilities and benefits to US military capability of the submarine transfer, as well as highlighting the division-of-labour option. As of this writing, no decision had been made on the restoration of funding for a second boat.[34] Worryingly for Australia, when the time comes for the United States to sell us the promised submarines there will not be any spare submarines available unless something very unlikely and unpredictable happens to speed up production. This is a known risk. At his US Senate confirmation hearing for a senior Pentagon position, Elbridge Colby expressed reservations about the wisdom of transferring any submarines to Australia when the United States might need them for the defence of Taiwan. The US failure to meet its own submarine build requirements is a reality that the Australian government continues to ignore. Australia is at the mercy of the United States and the personality and priorities of the American president as to whether or not it receives the promised submarines, and it has no leverage over what its ally decides to do.[35]

Making the odds of success even longer is the fact that the Royal Navy's submarine infrastructure is in even worse shape than that of the United States, which puts a big question mark on the plan to have the United Kingdom design the SSN-AUKUS. Peter Briggs, a retired RAN submarine specialist, calls Australia's reliance on the United Kingdom for its future boats 'profoundly disturbing' due to decades of inadequate design, difficult maintenance, poor crewing and bad sailor morale, as well as a major industrial contraction following the end of the Cold War that saw a highly skilled workforce go from 13 000 to 3000.[36] While the extent of the damage resulting from a major fire at the Barrow-in-Furness Shipyard on 30 October 2024, the UK's sole submarine construction facility, is not fully known, it may add more delay to an already stressed production system. Australia's 2024 donation of A$4.6 billion to prop up the British nuclear submarine industry is a peculiar act in light of the challenges outlined here, but one that the Albanese government believes it had little choice to make if the AUKUS plan is to have any chance of working.[37]

Third, Australia is placing another and even bigger bet that advances in subsurface detection technology will not make its future submarines visible to a suite of anti-submarine sensors and platforms within their operational life. Unfortunately for those who sail beneath the waves, sensor technology continues to improve. At present, nuclear-powered submarines have an advantage over conventional ones because they do not have to come near the surface to snorkel air in order to recharge their batteries. This makes it harder for anti-submarine warships, aircraft and sensors to find a nuclear boat. However, a 2015 report by the Center for Strategic and Budgetary Assessment anticipates that rapid increases in computer processing power, combined with rapidly advancing artificial intelligence techniques, will spur dramatic changes in undersea warfare. New sensor technologies that exploit nonsound-based techniques are maturing rapidly. Such devices include ones that can detect large metal undersea structures from the disturbance they create in the earth's electromagnetic field, such as a submarine's ferromagnetic hull, while others can distinguish between the acoustic wave created by a human object and a marine animal at a great distance. Sensors can now detect the tiny amount of radiation a nuclear submarine emits or the light they reflect from laser LED pulses. A 2020 report from the Australian National University predicts that detection technologies will reach the point where the ocean becomes transparent by the 2050s. Another study's preliminary findings suggest that warming oceans, due to climate change, will modify the transmission of sound underwater in a way that may make it easier to locate submarines. Additionally, the proliferation of uncrewed maritime platforms will increase the number of submarine hunters and sensors available to the opposition and at a much lower cost.[38] As one commentor asks, 'Does the landmark AUKUS deal make sense in an age of increased ocean transparency?'[39]

The year 2050 – if not sooner – is still well within the operational life expectancy of our nuclear-powered submarines, and if ocean transparency was to occur, Australia would have lost a very expensive bet. The bet is even more costly because uncrewed subsurface systems are also maturing rapidly and may be able to undertake many of the missions Australia expects its nuclear boats to perform. In fact, the prognosis for a submarine to avoid detection through silence will become so bleak that a 2023 study suggests that flooding the ocean with noise and hiding in static, not silence, may be the better tactic.[40]

The final factor concerns operational availability. Even if Australia was to obtain all eight nuclear-powered submarines, and if it had crews for all of them, which is unlikely given the RAN's current rate of recruitment and a Virginia boat's crew size being double that of a Collins boat, there would probably be only two or three available for operations at any one time. It is a well-accepted principle that it takes three or four submarines to generate one for deployment.[41] Two or three boats are not a lot of muscle with which to cover all the maritime approaches to Australia, protect maritime trade, hunt hostile submarines and deter a potential aggressor with China's level of power. Each Virginia submarine carries just twelve Tomahawk missiles and even if all were fired at once, one imagines the effect on China's decision-makers would be negligible. If we were bold enough to add the Tomahawks that will possibly be carried by the even more exposed Hobart and Hunter warships, the resulting additional firepower seems hardly worth the effort. In sum, Australia is spending a lot of money to obtain a very small capability that a potential aggressor will not take seriously – it is delusional thinking.

One of the main justifications Marles has offered for the surface fleet build-up is the need to secure Australia's sea lanes of communication. A defence media release dated 20 February 2024 noted that 'Navy's future fleet will be integral to ensure the safety and security of our sea lines of communication and maritime trade'. The media release included attributable quotes that stressed the importance of trade protection, including two from the Minister for Defence:

> Australia's modern society and economy rely on access to the high seas: trade routes for our imports and exports, and the submarine cables for the data which enables our connection to the international economy.

And:

> The Royal Australian Navy must be able to ensure the safety and security of our sea lines of communication and trade routes as they are fundamental to our way of life and our prosperity.[42]

The *NDS* simplifies the language by stating one of its goals as 'protecting Australia's critical sea lines of communication'.[43]

Marles's words cannot be taken at face value – at best, he is being disingenuous as to the feasibility of the RAN to protect the nation's trade. A basic outline of how Australia's exports and imports move across the seas reveals the impossibility of the RAN's task. According to the Department of Foreign Affairs and Trade, Australia's two-way trade in calendar year 2022 was A$1.2 trillion. The single largest trading partner was China – A$299 billion – which represented 24.9 per cent of the total. It appears highly improbable that the RAN will have reason to protect this trade if war with China eventuates, as it would cease in its entirety. The next two trading partners are Japan (12.3 per cent) and the United

States (7.3 per cent), closely followed by the Republic of Korea (6.8 per cent). The United Kingdom's share was the thirteenth largest at 2.1 per cent. With the exception of New Zealand (2.6 per cent share) all of Australia's trade links are long, and many require ships to sail within close proximity of Chinese waters.[44]

All of Australia's sea lines of communication are exposed for much of their length. The same can be said for Australia's undersea cables, which span the width of oceans in order to provide communications to Asia, Europe, North America and elsewhere. Australia plans to buy up to eleven Tier 2 general-purpose frigates whose primary task will be to protect the nation's trade and communications. The dilemma for the four or so ships that are available for service at any one time is, which part of the lines of communication do they patrol? For example, do they escort tankers from the Middle East on their voyage to Korean, Japanese, Singaporean or Chinese refineries, or do they protect the refined product as it sails to Australia? How does the RAN clear choke points such as the Lombok Strait of enemy mines, now that the 2024 *IIP* has cancelled the navy's mine clearance vessels? Even with the planned fleet expansion, Australia will not have enough surface vessels for a trade protection mission, nor the means to remove mines and other submerged hazards, such as autonomous subsurface vessels.

Fortunately, it is questionable as to whether an Australian warship will ever perform a trade protection mission, due to the fact that Australia does not have a merchant fleet of its own and cannot compel the merchant ships of other nations to carry its cargoes. Nearly all of Australia's international trade is carried on container, tanker and bulk cargo ships that are owned by international companies and registered overseas. In 2022, the Albanese government announced its intention to explore the acquisition of twelve merchant ships to serve as a national fleet.[45] While a good intention, the government's ambition of twelve vessels needs to be seen in context – in 2021 there were over 6170 foreign-flagged arrivals at Australian ports.[46] In mid-2023, the Department of Infrastructure issued a report on the national fleet's prospects, but it is not clear if there has been further progress.[47]

If war breaks out, the companies that own these ships may decide to not sail for Australian ports rather than risk their vessels. For these companies, there are alternative routes on which to make money rather than continuing with their Australian trade, or they may opt to take longer routes, which will increase sailing costs and delay delivery. The government may need to provide shipping firms with inducements to offset the risks.

Most of Australia's imports arrive inside a container. International maritime trade for container ships is highly concentrated, and the five largest companies control over 65 per cent of global shipping capacity. Compounding Australia's shipping difficulties is that the third largest marine container company in the world is COSCO Shipping, a Chinese company headquartered in Shanghai, which controls 12.5 per cent of the world's capacity. Presumably, these vessels would become unavailable to Australia in the case of war with China. In addition, modern trade practice is organised around shipping hubs, and cargo usually does not move directly between two ports unless it is a major route. Instead, containers are offloaded at hubs and reloaded onto other ships in order to create the most efficient consignment. Unfortunately for Australia, the world's largest hub in 2022 was Shanghai, with several other Chinese ports in the top ten.[48]

Bulk carriage ownership is less concentrated than it is for the container trade, but all of the industry's main players are based overseas and the ships are beyond Australia's control.[49] The other factor in Australia's bulk exports is that the top destination is China. In 2022, Australia's bulk exports totalled A$424 billion. Of this, $A123 billion (29.1 per cent) was with China. Another 34.2 per cent sailed for Japan, South Korea and Taiwan, whose ports are within range of interdiction by Chinese forces.[50] It is the same situation for liquid fuels. Australia's petroleum imports arrive in foreign-owned and -registered ships whose home ports are all overseas.

Presumably, the RAN will be working with other coalition partners to secure trade routes, but these partners will have their own trade to protect and will also need to secure merchant ships for their own needs. Trade may be important to Australia, but by world standards its trade routes are relatively small and out of the way when compared to the more concentrated trade routes in other parts of the world. What one should conclude from this brief trade outline is that the justification for buying the general-purpose frigates as recommended by the *ELSCF* report, and one of the rationales for getting nuclear-powered submarines, is weak.

A final matter that should be of concern for those who sail on Australia's future warships is that land-based missiles and small uncrewed attack boats are enjoying increasing success. It is unlikely that the Houthi irregulars will sink a warship in the Red Sea, but they are certainly keeping a flotilla of escort ships busy, and have had some success against merchant ships. Perhaps even more illustrative, Ukraine has sunk or disabled numerous Russian ships in the Black Sea with missiles and uncrewed vessels. We can imagine what a more advanced anti-ship network, such as that possessed by China, could do.

The core problem with the plan for the RAN's future is that it suffers from a number of poor judgements. They are:

1 That the future RAN plan was decided on in the absence of a grand strategy. This is another Defence example of acquisition occurring with little understanding of the art of the possible. The RAN cannot perform the tasks it will be given without being destroyed by a vastly more powerful enemy. Industrial policy, not national security policy, is the driving force behind the government's warship acquisition plans. Unfortunately, the government's priority for the future RAN is to secure the

ongoing employment of Osborne and Henderson shipyard workers rather than the more important responsibility of providing for the nation's protection.

2 That the government insists that the Chinese threat is urgent, yet opts for platforms that will not enter service for many years if not decades.
3 If deterrence fails, the RAN is poorly placed to succeed in combat against a capable opponent such as China. Instead of pursuing an asymmetric way of war, the government plans to build a fleet optimised to wage battle in a symmetrical style against a much stronger adversary. This is almost guaranteed to end very badly for the RAN and Australia.
4 That the insistence on trade as a core interest does not stand up to scrutiny when faced with the reality of the nation's international trade position.
5 That the RAN acquisition plan has been formulated with little, if any, consideration of non-traditional ways to achieve maritime power, nor any recognition that sea control can now be achieved from the land and the air. One cannot help wondering what the recommendations would have been if the *ELSCF* team had included one of the Ukrainians who had responsibility for transforming the Black Sea into a Russian no-sail zone.

I realise that the assessment in this section may appear on the harsh side. I also realise that the expectation is that the RAN fleet will once again be subsumed into a US-led task force. Still, preparing for war should not tolerate sentimentality or reverence for the status quo and should not undervalue courageous thinking and direct language. In a rapidly evolving security environment, it is insufficient and likely self-defeating for Australia to do more of the same. This section will now turn to what the RAN actually needs to do to meet its responsibilities for the security of the nation.

In 2013, the RAN's Sea Power Centre–Australia published my paper, 'The End of Maritime Strategy'.[51] I argued that the improving lethality of land-based long-range strike systems and the proliferation of sensors would make large warships obsolete. In a future in which the maritime environment will be dominated by land-based and air-launched missiles as well as maritime and aerial drone systems, the age of the surface and subsurface warship is coming to an end. As we have seen, in the ensuing years the capabilities of missiles, uncrewed systems and drones has only gotten better, while the cost of sinking or damaging a ship has declined. I am not the only one pointing out this trend. From an American point of view, retired USN officers, the late Captain Wayne P Hughes and Rear Admiral Robert Girrier, believe that as missiles improve and uncrewed systems proliferate, ships will need to become smaller. Large ships are just bigger targets.[52] American defence academic TX Hammes recognises that 'land-based antiship systems are dominating the surface of the sea out to ever increasing ranges'. The adage, attributed to Admiral Horatio Nelson, Hammes notes, '"A ship's a fool to fight a fort," remains true – but now extends to ever greater ranges from shore'.[53] The lesson here is that it is pointless to go to the trouble and expense of building costly and vulnerable warships with which to control the sea, when land- and air-based systems can do the same job at a much lower cost, both in taxpayer funds and human lives.

The RAN is at an inflection point in the art of war. Just as the battleship gave way to carrier aviation and the horse to mechanisation, the warship will cede primacy to long-range strike systems. Nor is it just the RAN that will have to change. The heart of the USN's maritime strike concept is the aircraft carrier group. Anti-access/area-denial technologies like those mounted by China risk turning today's carriers, like the battleships of old, into big, expensive white elephants that are too vulnerable to be put into harm's way.[54] As a RAND study observes, 'It is hard to think of a persuasive reason why aircraft carriers can defy technological progress when battleships could not'.[55] Large warships are legacy systems from an earlier age, an age that is coming to an end, and the RAN should take note.[56] Contemporary evidence of the ability of a land force to control the sea is becoming increasingly evident. The war in Ukraine periodically reminds us of the advantage missiles and drones have over ships. In a raid on Sevastopol in March 2024, Ukrainian uncrewed systems damaged four Russian landing craft. Admittedly, these ships were in port and not moving on the open sea, when one would expect protection to be greater, but Ukraine also sank the Russian Black Sea's flagship, the *Moskva*, while it was underway.[57]

The RAN's future does not lie with crewed platforms. The government should cancel all the acquisitions it has recently announced. Otherwise, they will be rendered useless by the shift in the character of maritime war. Australia also does not need such vessels in order to become a Strategic Defensive state. This does not mean the RAN should cease to exist. Sailors will still be required, as will warships. However, the warships will be uncrewed surface and subsurface vessels that are controlled from shore-based installations, aircraft or small command ships. In fact, as submersibles improve it may even become possible to dispense with surface fleets in their entirety. Australia's objective as it responds to the China challenge should be to secure the approaches to the nation's shores. To become a Strategic Defensive–minded maritime state no longer requires a fleet of large crewed warships. Sea control is not the end point of a maritime campaign, it is the means by which to secure the government's policy objective.[58] If the Australian government's objective is to protect the country, sea control and sea denial can be done without crewed warships.

A component of the RAN's build-up is the political choice to maintain the Henderson and Osborne shipyards. Yet the coming end of the crewed fleet does not mean these workers have to end up on the scrap heap. Instead, they can build the needed uncrewed vessels, as well as drones, and not in ones and twos, but in the thousands. An Australian military that can seed the waters to the country's north with thousands of uncrewed systems will be able to deny and sink enemy ships at much less risk and cost than it could via crewed platforms. If Australia wants a military shipbuilding industry, it should be one that is part of the future not the past.

The RAN will still need some crewed ships, but these will be types that will not sit at the heart of the nation's maritime combat system. At least in the short term, the RAN will need surface and subservice tenders and mother ships that will carry, launch and maintain the uncrewed fleet. These will need to be as small and stealthy as possible and should be considered expendable. Australia will also need transport ships in order to deploy the land force, although these can only venture forth into benign environments or where friendly distant strike assets have secured access. The additional benefit of the uncrewed concept is that it solves the RAN's interminable recruitment issue. The RAN will still need sailors, because even uncrewed vessels need people to control them from afar, but the recruitment pressure should ease because the terms of service will be more attractive and the required skill sets more readily available in the nation's workforce.

Some may view an uncrewed RAN as a radical idea. It is not. Rather, it is the logical end point of the precision strike and sensor revolution. It also has the advantage of countering China with an asymmetric way of war instead of attempting to fight a more powerful adversary head-on in its area of strength, while also having greater utility for climate-change conflicts. Instead, what the RAN is building is the perfect fleet for a stronger adversary to sink with relative ease. To go uncrewed meets the requirements of the philosophy of the Strategic Defensive – a navy that is designed to defend and impose costs on an adversary while minimising the risk to itself. In military technology, change does not accommodate fools. Australia can build an RAN fit for the future, or it can see the service destroyed.

The future Royal Australian Air Force

Each of the services had to give up something in the *IIP* in order to free up funds for the SSN program. For the RAAF the price was the fourth squadron of the F-35A Lightning II and the $4.5 billion its acquisition represented. It also means that despite the *NDS*'s promise of force projection there will be no expansion of the RAAF's combat capability, except for upgrades to existing platforms and the integration of new missiles.[59] That this appears contradictory is correct. The absence of any growth in strike aircraft dooms the RAAF to meeting a changing future of uncertainty and danger by remaining essentially the same. Unfortunately, the government has shown little ability to embrace new ideas when it comes to the air domain.

The *DSR* recommended just two additions to RAAF capability, which the *IIP* later confirmed. The first is the integration of the Long-Range Anti-Ship Missile onto the F-35 and F/A-18F Super Hornet aircraft. The F-35 is also to receive the Joint Strike Missile. The second recommendation concerns the MQ-28A Ghost Bat, the RAAF's uncrewed aircraft that is designed to team with the RAAF's crewed platforms. As of March 2024, the Ghost Bat's manufacturer, Boeing, had begun construction of a production facility in Queensland, although the *IIP* provided approved monies of only $280 million. The remaining $4 to $5 billion required over the tenure of the *IIP* is listed as an 'unapproved planned investment'. Both recommendations are sensible and important additions to RAAF capability, and hopefully the government will buy all three in more than bespoke numbers.

However, the RAAF's overall program does not make the grade, thanks to a lack of imagination on the part of defence policy-makers and the force's senior leaders. In the precision age, missiles are the critical weapon with which to strike a distant target, particularly against an opponent that has an integrated air defence system. The number of missiles a military is able to launch is important, and more is better.

Instead of embracing divergent thinking, the RAAF hamstrings itself by continuing to limit its definition of air combat capability to its fast jets, while ignoring the ability of the other aircraft it flies to carry missiles. The government is similarly culpable by allowing this to happen. A big change for the future of air power is that it is now possible to use the RAAF's transport fleet of C-17A Globemaster III and C130J-30 Hercules aircraft as missile launchers. Both of these planes have impressive endurance and long ranges, are able to fly at high ceilings – although admittedly not quite as lofty as the fast jets – and can carry lots of cargo in the form of missiles. They are actually more suitable than the F-35 to carry out an air strike mission against a distant target. The RAAF's other large aircraft, such as the P8A-Poseidon, can also carry missiles underwing, but not in the numbers that a cargo plane can hold internally. As a missile platform, transporters outperform what the RAAF defines as its attack aircraft. Table 5.2 compares the specifications of the RAAF's transport fleet with its fast jets.

Table 5.2
RAAF transporter specifications as a missile platform compared to fast jets[60]

Aircraft	Range	Payload	Ceiling
C-17A Globemaster (transport)	10,390 km	70 tonnes	45,000 feet
C-130J-30 Hercules (transport)	6,852 km (no payload)	19.5 tonnes	40,000 feet
F35-A Lightning II (fast jet)	2,200 km	8.1 tonnes	50,000 feet
F/A-18F Super Hornet (fast jet)	2,700 km	Figure not provided by RAAF	50,000 feet

The idea is that when a transport aircraft reaches its launch point, the crew opens the cargo ramp, palletised missiles roll out the back, the missiles separate, ignite and head to their targets. The USAF has already demonstrated the feasibility of this concept in a program it calls Rapid Dragon.[61] Importantly, the concept does not require any modification to the aircraft, and missile deployment is via standard drop procedures.

Presumably the RAAF is watching the development of Rapid Dragon. Perhaps it is quietly doing experimentation of its own. One hopes so, since this appears to be an easy win. Success will require some adjustment to the ethos of the RAAF, however. Military organisations contain status hierarchies and in the RAAF the pinnacle is occupied by the fast jet pilot. If the RAAF were to adopt the Rapid Dragon concept, the transport pilot would become the main enabler of kinetic effect from the air, which fast jet pilots are certain to not like. However, there are numerous other benefits that should encourage the RAAF to use its transports as missile launchers. The transport fleet offers the ability to launch many more missiles from a single aircraft, thereby saturating a target's defences. The transporters also have three to five times more range than the fast jets, enabling them to strike far more distant targets without the need for aerial refuelling. Transport aircraft are cheaper to buy and maintain than fast jets and the C-130 and C-17 are mature designs from which defects have been largely eliminated. Most importantly, the skills required to fly a transport aircraft are less advanced than those needed for a fast jet, which translates into a lower training requirement and a larger potential pool of aircrew. One can even foresee the C-130 flying uncrewed in the not-too-distant future. One of the intractable problems of all three services is the recruitment and retention of highly skilled individuals. Anything that reduces the training load and widens the defence recruitment pool has major benefits for the ADF.

In its pursuit of the Strategic Defensive, Australia needs to bring to bear against its opponent as much firepower as it can. Because it is likely to be the weaker power, Australia needs to be imaginative in how it develops asymmetric techniques with which to gain an advantage against the enemy. The Albanese government has already ordered twenty C-130J Hercules to replace the existing twelve. But this is not a simple replacement of tired aircraft with fresh ones. The new C130s will come with an advanced electronic warfare fit that is similar to one carried by the USAF's MC-130J II, the Hercules special operations variant. The Australian aircraft will have superb ability to penetrate hostile airspace, which will make them highly suitable for a bombing role, especially when escorted by the F-35 and the EA-18G Growler. The only bad news in this purchase is that the government has only ordered twenty. It should order as many as the Americans will allow.[62] Launching missiles from transporters also helps solve one of the deficiencies of the RAN – that is, the relatively low missile capability of its warships. Instead of sending an expensive and vulnerable ship to deny the enemy access to the sea, Australia can send a plane. The *IIP* does not contain any information on the RAAF's other transport aircraft, the C-27J Spartan. Presumably it will continue to serve.

The future Australian Army

Despite the recommended cutting of the second regiment of self-propelled howitzers and a reduction in the number of infantry fighting vehicles that the land force is to acquire, the *DSR*, *NDS* and *IIP* hold real promise for the Army.[63] Past defence reviews, such as *The Defence of Australia* white paper of 1987, marginalised the Army and assigned it a mission that was little more than a constabulary role: it tasked the land force with rounding up enemy personnel who managed to evade the RAN and RAAF and reach

Australia's shores. This time, the Army has received strategic-level roles on par with the other services.

The two tasks given to the Army are to dominate the approaches to Australia with land-based long-range fires based on a truck-mounted missile system, and to structure itself in order to be capable of littoral manoeuvre. The Army is to receive the US High Mobility Artillery Rocket System (HIMARS) and has been told to expand the procurement. To enable littoral manoeuvre, the government has instructed the Army to increase and accelerate the acquisition of its new landing craft and boats so that the land force can again cross open seas and operate in coastal and riverine waters. Both programs are moving forward.

Littoral manoeuvre requires the ability to conduct operations on the water, project force from the land over the water, or project force from the sea onto the land. It also includes the forward movement of long-range fires in order to extend the range of these systems.[64] For the Army this will require a different way of looking at manoeuvre. Not since the Second World War have the coastal waters to Australia's north been perceived as a highway through which to facilitate manoeuvre. The Army has begun the process of reorganising its formations in order to develop the requisite littoral capabilities. This new tasking also means that the Army will have to turn the page on two decades of low-intensity fighting against terrorists and insurgents, and again focus on how to fight a powerful state-based adversary.[65]

This is a promising start for the land force, but the government then fails to match promise with reality. A key problem for the land force is that all the recent Defence policy documents have seemingly overlooked a critical requirement which, if not corrected, will render much of the Army's role moot in a future war. At present, the Army does not have the right to conduct any littoral manoeuvres to the north because these islands and waters belong to other countries. I have to assume that the document's authors realise this, which makes the situation even worse because it suggests an element of colonial-era mindset is present in the littoral manoeuvre ambitions of the *DSR* and *NDS*. For this plan to be realised, Australia will need the permission of the other countries in the region before violating their sea space, a legal necessity that also applies to overflights of foreign territory by the RAAF or sailings by the RAN into someone else's waters. The government needs to fix this – it is not an Army or ADF problem to solve. The reality, at present, is that if the Army were to land a HIMARS launcher on a foreign shore it could be seen as an act of war by the territory's owner. At best it would see the Australian troops interned and their weapons confiscated. Moreover, such an act might go against the foreign policy interests of the country whose territory Australia has violated. Jakarta, Suva and Port Moresby might not want to get involved in a war between Australia and China.

If the ADF were to obtain territorial access to the littoral coast to Australia's north, an even more intractable problem remains: the ADF's limited power projection capability. For example, if China obtained a base in these waters, with or without the local country's permission, the government might task the ADF with its eviction. Such a mission would require a heavy combat capability – tanks, infantry fighting vehicles and artillery – considerable sea lift and significant logistic support. The latter, never available in abundance in the ADF, has been made even more challenging by the *IIP*'s cancellation of the RAN's support ship acquisition.

Presumably, the Chinese garrison would be in the order of a PLA Navy Marine combined arms battalion with attached armour, artillery, aviation and other elements. In addition, the base would likely contain maritime strike defences and surface-to-air missile launchers. To shift a force of this size and complexity, which nonetheless by Chinese standards is not very large – there are eighteen PLA Navy Marine combined arms battalions on the order of battle – would require the Army to commit a force on the order of a brigade plus – which is essentially its entire offensive capability. It seems very unlikely that the government would put into harm's way all of its deployable land force along with its naval escort and risk their destruction.

The fact remains that the Army is too small for the tasks the government is likely to assign to it in a hostile littoral, a fact that the authors of the *DSR* and *NDS* have overlooked. Unless the Army is made bigger and more powerful, and the RAN is able to provide a more robust escorting task force, as well as continuous air cover from the RAAF, any littoral manoeuvre above the size of a special forces surveillance patrol is fantasy. Unfortunately, the *IIP* does little for those combat arms that must close with and defeat an enemy in battle. This means the Army will remain a boutique force of highly trained elements that are too small to achieve an effect without assistance from the US military.

The government's decision to increase the Army's HIMARS acquisition to forty-two units is welcome, although this is a minimal amount. Sometime in the near future the Australian Army will also receive the Precision Strike Missile (PrSM), which recently entered service with the US Army. Both missiles have a maximum range of 500 kilometres and conveniently use the same launcher. The PrSM will only be able to target land-based targets, at least initially. Australia intends to manufacture both missiles in Australia and progress is being made to do so. Land-based long-range strike is the least costly way to launch a missile and offers the largest economic differential between the value of the missile dispatched and the target destroyed.

The government describes HIMARS and PrSM as long-range systems, but the maximum strike distance for both missiles is only about 500 kilometres. This means they are effectively tactical systems on the modern battlefield where operational ranges are measured in the thousands of kilometres. While HIMARS and PrSM will greatly increase the Army's existing strike range, it is not anywhere near enough. As already noted, the presumed enemy –

China – already has missiles in service that have much greater ranges. This means Australia's missile systems will have to get within the enemy's strike zone before they are able to shoot. The Australia launcher will probably not survive the attempt. The only solution is for the ADF to consider a ballistic missiles program because only these weapons actually have the range needed to hold the enemy at risk, as the government intends in the *NDS*.[66]

In addition, the Army should examine the feasibility of mounting its launchers on platforms other than trucks. In 2020, I published a paper that argued for the inclusion of a missile launcher capability on the littoral manoeuvre watercraft that the Army was developing.[67] Small boats and ships that can carry a missile-launching truck or trailer increase the flexibility of Australia's Strategic Defensive potential. Moreover, the Army should be exploring the possibility of obtaining containerised missile systems that can be placed on any flat surface of sufficient size. They can even be air-dropped to a forward element, fired and forgotten. This technology is evolving rapidly. For example, the US Navy has experimented with firing the Standard Missile (SM)-6 from a container mounted on a littoral combat ship. The Russian Kaliber cruise missile container system is operational. It should be possible for the Australian Army to fire a containerised missile from a barge, vehicle ferry or even the deck of the RAN's two amphibious ships.

All of the recent defence policy documents contain a glaring gap in their recommendations that defies explanation, especially in light of the wars that are presently being waged. The *IIP* contains a trivial amount of money for the Army to accelerate and expand its ownership of drones – only $190 million in approved investment, and between $500 and $700 million in unapproved investment, over the decade.[68] Even stranger is the absence of anything regarding the urgency of acquiring counter-drone systems. The ambitions of Army's recently announced counter-drone acquisition program – Land 156 – was limited to market analysis, and the land force remains a long way from fielding any defensive systems.[69] This deficiency is sadly consistent with the scant attention the *IIP* gives to uncrewed systems for the RAN and RAAF.

It is always risky to draw lessons from ongoing conflicts because not only is there as yet no resolution, but the information available is often incomplete and can be one-sided. That said, a ready takeaway from the wars in Ukraine, Yemen and Gaza is that uncrewed systems of all types are rapidly increasing in capability and lethality. The age in which, if you are seen, a drone will kill you has arrived. In Ukraine and the Red Sea, all sides are using drones to inflict casualties, and destroy equipment, vehicles and infrastructure.

Since the wars in Iraq and Afghanistan, the Australian Army has operated some uncrewed aerial systems. When I worked in Army Headquarters, a robotic dog would periodically stroll down the corridor, and there has been good progress in converting M113 Armoured Personnel Carriers to remote-controlled operation. Yet the period for experimentation is rapidly passing. The ADF cannot wait until drones become a mature technology with stable and predictable production lines and the industry consolidates around a few main manufacturers. Instead, the ADF should strive to shape the industry to its needs and convince the government to embrace drones and purchase them in very large numbers. Such is the importance of these devices that the government should consider supporting a domestic industry for their manufacture and further development, and thereby realise a sovereign industry that has more utility to the private sector than warship building. As a matter of urgency, it is also necessary to obtain the means to defeat enemy drones, for which the battlefields of Ukraine illustrate some possibilities. There has been some movement in this direction. The Army recently purchased the prototype for a laser-based anti-drone system. Perhaps the next step would be to buy the company.[70]

Within the defence commentariat community there is opposition to the Army acquiring heavy vehicles such as the Abrams tank or the Redback infantry fighting vehicle. This opposition is misplaced. Alluding to the destruction of various tanks in Ukraine misses the point. People die in war, because war is highly destructive. To reduce death to one's own side, a force must either become very good at hiding or at force protection. Armoured vehicles are vulnerable, but imagine the carnage that would result during an enemy barrage if soldiers were not inside one. Nothing in contemporary history suggests that land combat is coming to an end or that some mysterious force has given Australia an exemption from the need to take part in it. Australia could get away without heavy armour when it fought terrorists, but this will not be the case when it confronts a more powerful foe.[71]

The rise of long-range strike also holds some significance for the hierarchy within the Army. Primacy has belonged to the infantry in the Australian Army since the campaign in the Pacific in the Second World War. In the combined arms system, it has been the infantry that has stood at the forefront, because it has been the infantry that occupied the objective. As the Army transitions to a distant fires and littoral force, the infantry soldier will remain important, and will continue to be the element that seizes ground – but sometimes there will be no need to seize ground. The mission may only need a missile gunner to destroy a target from a distance and that target need not be on the land. In addition, the manoeuvre force will need the missile and tube gunners, to soften up the target and suppress the enemy's fires so that it can advance onto and through the objective. Under these conditions, the need to manoeuvre across the littoral to take objectives will not go away, but it will be less important than previously because the missile gunner can dissuade the enemy without even seeing them. It is the long-range strike platforms that will deny the enemy access to Australia and the region.

There is also another cultural shift that the Army will need to make to secure its place in a Strategic Defensive–focused ADF. At present, the dominant element within the Army is the full-time force, whereas the reserve, or part-time force, is the lesser element. This was not always the case. After Federation the government opted for a nearly total part-time land force with the only full-time element being those who staffed the coastal defences or who served as headquarters staff and instructors. If Australia adopted the philosophy of the Strategic Defensive, the main element of the force could again be its part-timers. The only full-time forces would be those who staffed and maintained the coastal defence force – missiles and drones – as well as staff, trainers and a small standing force that would be needed at short notice. Reservists would be mobilised as needed, either to strengthen the defences against a potential threat or to participate in a deployment to a climate-torn war zone. While this policy change might sound dramatic, it is simply the best way to meet the security requirements of a Strategic Defensive state, and a return to the force's origins.

The future of the space and cyber domains

Not a lot can be said about the cyber domain because so little is known about Australia's capabilities and intentions in this area. The Strategic Defensive easily incorporates cyber into its philosophy, however. For example, the ADF could employ a cyber strike on an adversary's command and control or sensor networks to disrupt its operations. Similarly, using cyber to corrupt the enemy's intelligence collection and data processing could impose decision-making constraints on its commanders. Australia should continue to develop its capabilities across the cyber domain, as well as harden its military systems and civilian infrastructure against attack.

Australia's Space Command celebrated its third anniversary in January 2025.[72] Although a relatively new entity, the exploitation of space for military purposes has been underway for some time in other countries – the USAF launched its first communications satellite in 1958. Australia has been a relative laggard in the space domain, largely because the ADF has been able to leverage US capabilities.

With the release of the *IIP* it was clear that the government was supportive of the expansion of the ADF's space capabilities and had established a pathway for its development. Despite the lack of detail, the government in the *IIP* allocated large sums for the domain's advancement: $4.5 billion in approved planned investment and $22 to $31 billion in unapproved planned investment. However, within months the government seemingly changed its mind. In early November 2024, Defence announced the withdrawal of its tender for and the cancellation of Joint Program 9102, a satellite communication program. The Defence media release offered the rationale that a single orbit system would not meet 'requirements for contemporary and future capability', although only a few months earlier it had.[73] Joint Program 9102 had a price tag of approximately $7 billion, which presumably will be repurposed.[74] The government has not announced what will replace this program, if anything. As far as is known, funding for DEF-799, a geo-intelligence project, has continued. [75]

It is hard to gauge what the cancellation of the satellite purchase means for the development of the ADF's space capability. This is because of the necessary secrecy any space programs attract. We have to assume the government has a plan and that the rationale for this cancellation was not driven simply by the need to provide money for the SSN acquisition, because even submarines require communications.

Hopefully, the government will provide more information in the near future, because space, as a military domain, will continue to develop since it plays such a vital role in enabling the other domains of war. It is also an important factor in any Strategic Defensive state as it allows the military to identify and strike at targets that threaten the nation. Many military systems rely upon space to function effectively, including communications, surveillance and targeting. Space is the modern era's high ground, and its control enables a combatant to see what the other side is doing or planning to do. It is not clear at this time, at least not in the public domain, but the destination for Australia's space ambitions should be the ability to coordinate and integrate all ADF activities across all domains. To achieve this, Australia will require its own space launch capability, which a number of private companies are positioning themselves to provide.

Climate change and the Strategic Defensive

So far, this chapter has not said too much about what type of capabilities the ADF requires if it is to secure the nation from its other threat – climate change. In part, this is because I have had to respond to the future ADF that the government is planning, and the recent defence policy documents have little to say about climate change. It is also because some military capabilities are multi-purpose and can prove useful against more than one threat. Therefore, a few words specifically from the perspective of the Strategic Defensive response to climate change threats are in order.

That the *DRS*, *NDS* and *IIP* do not give serious consideration to climate change is certainly a major oversight since the risk from climate events will only grow as humanity continues to add greenhouse gases to the atmosphere. The principal events the ADF must prepare for are collapsed states and mass migrations. Regional wars will become more common as the effects of climate change destabilise nearby states and result in the likely emergence of territories that are essentially ungoverned. The ADF may find that its main role in the future is propping up climate change–affected states. Soldiers should expect to deploy into regional conflict zones in which desperate people are struggling to survive and in which there will be no friends. These operations will be unlike the relatively benign intervention in East Timor and more akin to Somalia in 1992 and Kosovo in 1998. There will be elements of warfighting, disaster relief and state building, all at the same time, and will require a land force, with maritime and air support, with the full suite of military capabilities.

Climate change is also expected to trigger large-scale migration. Some parts of the world are predicted to become uninhabitable as temperatures routinely exceed the level of human survivability. Moreover, with the collapse of agriculture, desperate people will have to make a decision: starve or move. At present, even relatively small migration movements are a cause of concern for the residents of the target state, for example the US southern border. Larger scale movements, perhaps comprising entire populations, will only increase the strain. At some point, the Australian public will need to make a decision. Will Australia welcome millions of refugees for whom there is no chance of ever returning home, or will they deny them entry? In either situation, the ADF will be required.

While there is a significant overlap between what the ADF needs to fight China and to manage climate change conflicts, there are some elements that are completely useless. Nuclear-powered submarines provide Australia with no benefit in a climate emergency, another reason to not acquire them. The RAN's large warships are similarly poor choices for a climate crisis, whereas smaller transport and support ships will prove essential and be needed in large numbers. The Army, which is the force that will find itself most heavily involved in separating warring bands in a collapsed state, will need to be larger. The RAAF's transport aircraft will similarly grow in utility, both for carrying aid supplies and as missile bombers, depending on the circumstances. The ADF's plans for its space capabilities remain critical because of their ability to provide decision-makers with essential information. For climate change conflict, the priority would be on numbers, depth of resources and flexibility of usage. The general conclusion, however, is that the ADF is too small and must become much larger if Australia is to secure its aims in a climate-disrupted future.

There is one further aspect of climate change that warrants consideration here. The ADF is often called upon to assist civil authorities when a flood, storm or bushfire strikes the community. Soldiers are activated to assist the state-based emergency organisations in managing the disaster. Personnel from the RAN and RAAF help too, but it is the Army that usually provides the majority of the numbers. It is very expensive to recruit, train and maintain soldiers (and sailors and aviators) for their primary task of waging war, and disaster response is a wasteful use of a scarce asset. There is a better way. The government should establish a federal disaster response organisation to supplement the state-based ones. Many of its members will be employed part time and called up when needed. More importantly, a core contingent of full-time staff would serve as planners charged with understanding where the risks lie and proposing solutions before disaster strikes. Climate change events are only going to get worse and if the ADF is to do its warfighting job properly it needs relief from the disaster response mission.

An integrated force

In the past, one of the goals the ADF routinely aspired to was to become a joint force. By joint it meant the RAN, Army and RAAF being able to operate together without impediment. Unfortunately, the ADF never achieved this goal, and operational jointness remains a distant promise. The reason for this failure is that when on operations, such as in Afghanistan or Iraq, ADF in-theatre force elements naturally aligned with their American counterparts rather than with each other. Deployed RAN ships sailed as part of a USN-led taskforce, RAAF planes were subsumed into the US-run air component system, and Army forces were attached to the relevant coalition ground command. Operational integration with the relevant US command was far more useful than for the Australian services to be able to work together as a joint force.[76]

The Australian military is now to become an integrated force. From a close reading of the *DSR* this appears to be an extension of jointness to the five current domains – sea, land, air, space and cyber. The *DSR* does not specify how integration is to occur, but does provide a long list of capabilities for which the ADF is to achieve operational integration. The *NDS* includes a large section on integration, but it is simply a list of the various capabilities the five domains will own. It does not explain how they are to become integrated.[77] That the *NDS* described integration as a list of domain-owned capabilities is an ominous start to the process of integration. When the US Army began to develop the idea of war without domain ownership, one of its observations was that to achieve integration you need to conceive of the result you want, not who owns the asset. Therefore, it would have been wiser for the authors of the *NDS* to list the effect sought and then speculate on how various combinations of integrated capabilities could achieve that outcome.

In addition, it is worth considering how the ADF can achieve success at integration now when the easier to achieve joint capability proved elusive, particularly as having the ability to operate with the United States remains a priority. After all, Marles has stated that his goal for the future of the alliance is to move beyond interoperability between the Australian and American militaries to the higher metric of interchangeability.[78] There is a conflict between ADF integration and US–Australian interchangeability, and achieving both seems improbable.

There is another risk in aiming for the level of integration that the *DSR* and *NDS* seek – hubris. In the 1990s, due to advances in sensors, precision strike and information processing, the US military aimed to achieve information dominance and battlefield transparency. The enemy would have nowhere to hide and US commanders would have all relevant information available to them. This became known as the Revolution in Military Affairs, a revolution that went on to failure on the battlefields of Iraq and Afghanistan. As an ambition, it displayed all of the worst features of the military's faith in technology to solve all problems, and the ability of highly intelligent people to delude themselves. It is too soon to know if a similar fate awaits the ADF regarding integration. Notwithstanding any of this, from the perspective of the Strategic Defensive, Australia's priority should always be to have its forces work together in the most efficient and effective method possible, and this should not require the invention of a new label. It would also be a good idea for those charged with this ambition to acquaint themselves with the American experience of the Revolution in Military Affairs.

Force protection

Australia is planning to spend very large sums of money on capabilities to deter potential Chinese aggression and to protect the global rules-based order. Yet amid the discussion on what to acquire, there has been little mention of how to protect these expensive new assets, or how to hide them from observation by Chinese satellites, aerial reconnaissance, or someone on a nearby hill or roof that overlooks an Australian military base. The February and March 2025 transit of Chinese warships in waters near Australia demonstrated their ability to operate in our neighbourhood. The *IIP* specifies zero money for physical protection, although it does allocate some funds for electronic warfare, which would include protecting the ADF's electronic capabilities from interference.[79] There is, unfortunately, nothing novel in this absence of thinking on force protection. The *2020 Force Structure Plan* summarised the spending of $575 billion, but also made no mention of how Defence was to protect or conceal its acquisitions.[80] In the same year, I published a piece in *The Strategist* that discussed the need to invest in defensive infrastructure and suggested that every new capability acquisition program include a protection component. I do not believe this has occurred. A lack of attention to the protection of Australia's defence capabilities is a perennial failure.[81]

The 2024 *IIP* calls for a total planned investment in the ADF's northern bases of between $14 and $18 billion over the period out to fiscal year 2033–4. However, the focus is on improving force *projection*, not force *protection*. Similarly, the *DSR* and the *NDS* contain no mention of how to protect the ADF's assets from enemy attack.[82] The principle that one has to actually have survivable assets in order to project power has been lost on the authors of these policy papers.

In an age of long-range precision strikes, all of Australia can be targeted by an adversary, particularly one with the strength of China. To date, however, Australia's aircraft continue to be parked out in the open or reside in ordinary and easily identified hangars, the RAN's ships and submarines tie up to wharves in the open air, and the Army's vehicles sit in uncovered parking lots on their bases. If war comes, Australia is in for a rude awakening, just as America was at Pearl Harbor and Manila in 1941. The first time the government learns that Australia is at war may be when reports arrive in Canberra of the smouldering ruins of the nation's ships, planes and vehicles.

Defence also needs to provide for the protection of its headquarters and even provide alternative secure locations. HQ Joint Operations Command sits in a paddock near the town of Bungendore in the New South Wales countryside, conveniently located alongside a rail line that serves as a targeting arrow. Defence's other main headquarters reside in the Russell Defence precinct in Canberra, a complex of office buildings across the lake from Parliament House. While these buildings are impossible to harden, there are other options, such as constructing facilities for key personnel deep underground or in specially excavated mountain caverns or other remote locations. Australia is currently building tunnels through the Snowy Mountains in order to extend the hydroelectric scheme.

Perhaps a tunnelling machine could also hollow out a few chambers that could be set aside for key defence personnel if ever required.

In addition to pouring concrete, the ADF needs to rediscover the ancient arts of deception and camouflage. Deception encourages the enemy to look in the wrong place, while camouflage hides what is there. They are complementary, and include both physical and electronic methods. In the Second World War, the Allies successfully implemented several deception plans that kept the Germans guessing where the British and Americans would land on D-Day. These included creating a non-existent army group, faking air drops using 'chaff', and spreading disinformation through networks of double agents. There was a time when the Australian military possessed dedicated camouflage units – they are again needed.

Australia is a big place and it should be possible to disperse and hide much of the ADF's equipment. Real or decoy road houses or storage buildings could contain a HIMARs launcher while aircraft rest under mock shelters or caverns cut into hillsides. The ADF will also need to learn how to fight dispersed, because to concentrate forces in an age of pervasive sensors is to invite destruction. The Swiss were masters of disguise and hollowed out mountains as storage depots while roads doubled as runways. Australia's relative weakness means it must hide its limited assets if it is to still possess them, intact, when they are required. The ADF needs to strive to deceive and hide because, as the war in Ukraine shows, once an asset is located, a missile, artillery round or drone soon arrives.

Nuclear weapons

Governments of both main parties have maintained that Australia is already in fact protected by nuclear weapons, they just happen to be US ones. Defence policy documents, starting with the *Strategic Review 1993*, assert that Australia is covered by America's program of extended nuclear deterrence. This means that if Australia were to be attacked by nuclear weapons, the United States would mount a nuclear response against the assailant on our behalf. Because of this commitment from the United States, Australia has no need to acquire a sovereign nuclear response capability.[83]

There is only one problem with the nuclear extended deterrence guarantee: the United States has never agreed to it. American policy-makers have never given any public commitment that Australia is among the countries it would support with nuclear weapons in case of attack. Japan has received such a commitment, but the best Australia can claim is that the United States has never objected whenever we assert this privilege. Of the major US allies, Australia is the only one lacking a formal extended deterrence dialogue. Perhaps there is a private guarantee, but it is worthless since it can be denied when convenient. America's refusal to state categorically that Australia is protected beneath its nuclear umbrella means that the United States reserves its decision to the moment that it is most needed. Statecraft is about a nation safeguarding its own interests, and here is an example of the United States doing just that. The reality is that it may or may not be in US interests to retaliate on Australia's behalf if the time comes.[84]

Nuclear weapons provide a nation with the ultimate defence. If attacked, a nation that possesses them can bring wholesale destruction down upon their aggressor and thereby impose risks that the leaders of a hostile state would almost certainly not be willing to run. Because of the potential for overwhelming destruction, nuclear weapons are a very powerful way to deter potential enemies. Every potential aggressor knows that they risk mutually assured destruction if they attack a rival who is so armed. To invite destruction offers no worthwhile policy objective, and war is all about achieving useful policy outcomes. The Cold War remained cold because both sides knew that there could be no winners. However, that happy outcome may have been more of an accident than the result of successful policy – deterrence theory may not be the panacea its enthusiasts claim.[85] This is because above all deterrence is a matter of psychology, and as Henry Kissinger argued, 'What the potential aggressor believes is more crucial than what is objectively true. Deterrence occurs above all in the minds of men'.[86]

While there can be no winners when going to war with a nuclear-armed opponent, there can be losers. Deterrence relies on a number of factors for which there is no guarantee. Most importantly it requires rational actors, yet human decision-making is shaped by both rational and emotional processes. Luckily to date, the responsibility for whether or not to employ nuclear weapons has fallen to rational actors. To succeed, deterrence also needs flawless technology that works as designed. Unfortunately, this has not always been the case, and there have been numerous close calls by both the Soviet Union and the United States. In 1983, Soviet military officer Stanislav Petrov, while the duty officer at a nuclear early-warning centre, reported to his superiors that its detection of a US launch was actually a system malfunction. Had he identified it as an actual attack the Soviets would have responded in kind, likely leading to nuclear annihilation as the two nations exchanged atomic blows.[87] Three years earlier, outside the small town of Damascus, Arkansas, a Titan II Intercontinental Ballistic Missile experienced a fuel leak. Several hours later, there was a massive explosion which ejected the missile from the silo. Fortunately, for the inhabitants of central Arkansas, its 9-megaton warhead did not detonate.[88] So far, humanity has had luck on its side; hopefully we will continue to do so.

Those who escape death from the nuclear firestorm and the radioactive fallout will then have to survive the ensuing nuclear winter. The burning of cities will send dust into the atmosphere that prevents sunlight from reaching the ground. In the aftermath of a nuclear exchange, temperatures decline rapidly, perhaps by as much as 10°C, plants become less productive and livestock die. No one is quite sure how many detonations are required to cause a nuclear winter but modelling suggests that even a modest exchange, such as one between India and Pakistan, would result in about two billion human deaths from starvation. How far the temperature drops and for how long is a variable dependent on the number of blasts, the size of the warheads used and the construction of the targets.[89]

At present, the Australian government intends to deter an aggressor by strengthening the ADF. If this desire is continued to its ultimate resolution, reasoning dictates that Australia should obtain nuclear weapons with which to defend itself. But in doing so, Australia would cross the threshold of an exclusive club of states that hold the power to destroy humanity. Personally, I have no desire to see Australia become a member of this club, but I am not the decision-maker. The limit of my input is to suggest the basis on how the decision should be made. If Australia decides to become a nuclear-armed state, it should only do so after the government determines that the total risk from an aggressor, such as China, up to and including the occupation of the continent, would be worse than the acceptance of possible destruction in a total war. An Australian nuclear arsenal, therefore, only makes sense if the government believes a war with China will be waged over existential, or 'total war', ambitions. If a nation's war goals are more limited, nuclear weapons are not justified. At present, there is no suggestion that China has any intentions towards Australia that come anywhere close to wanting our destruction. This suggests that a nuclear-armed Australia is not necessary. What would be useful, however, is clarity on the status of Australia's extended deterrence guarantee. This should be relatively easy to obtain – our prime minister should reach out to the American president and ask.

The American alliance

The ANZUS Alliance is now over seventy years old. This is a venerable agreement. Throughout its existence, the alliance has evolved in practice, but nothing has changed in the text. What began as a security treaty to placate Australia and New Zealand over the risk of a rearmed Japan has become a pact with global implications for the deployment of Australian military force. For the Australian government, the defence relationship with the United States is the most important security link imaginable. The government's security trend runs in only one direction – intensification.

That is a shame, because no alliance is foolproof. After seventy-plus years a review of the ANZUS Treaty is in order. I do believe the relationship has merit, despite the robust position this book takes on AUKUS and the nuclear submarine acquisition. But a relationship check-up is overdue. Despite their insistence that nothing has changed in the US relationship, Australia's political class must be cognisant of the hasty and ill-thought changes that Trump and his followers are imposing on the American alliance structure. Traditionally, its alliance structure is seen as America's greatest advantage over hostile states, but now it is coming under great strain as the US administration insults its friends, such as calling Poland's foreign minister a 'small man' and ordering him to 'be quiet'. Australia has not, as of this writing, been party to the treatment Trump has meted out to Europe, but it is probably only a matter of time. One hopes that in light of the strange and disturbing behaviour currently emanating from Washington, Australia's leaders have recognised that being a sub-imperial power may no longer be a viable security policy, but if so they are not giving anything away.

Australia's political leaders must admit that a new security environment has arrived and that the ANZUS alliance may not be as sacrosanct as they like to believe. They also need to be more honest with the Australian public about the cost and obligations they accept on the nation's behalf. By this, I do not mean the alacrity with which Australia joins a US-led war. Rather, the Australian government has allowed the alliance to become unbalanced to the point where it costs us more than it provides. Because of the alliance, Australian defence is based on US priorities not Australian ones, contributing to the following negative effects:

- Australia behaves like a Strategic Offensive state when it is a natural Strategic Defensive one.
- Australia avoids the development of a grand strategy because it follows the US lead.
- Australia is drawn, willingly and without much reflection, into wars of dubious legality.
- Australia looks to a distant imperial seat in defiance of its own geography.
- Australia avoids climate change as a security responsibility.
- Australia refuses to become a fully sovereign state.

While the above are all serious issues, I believe the main problem with the alliance is that it allows Australian governments to avoid treating national security with the intelligence, resoluteness and seriousness it deserves. For our political leaders, national security ultimately does not matter because if trouble ever presents itself the United States will back us, or at least that is the expectation. Attending to national security, in its broadest definition, is the government's most important responsibility to the Australian public. Yet the Australian government continues to off-load a huge component of this critical responsibility to another country. Whether or not nuclear-powered submarines arrive in some distant future, or if the Hobart- and Hunter-class warships are so undergunned as to be useless, are apparently not points of central concern to the government. If they were, the government would not proceed with its current plans.

In ceding to the United States most of the military component of our national security, the government fails to allow the nation to develop as a truly independent sovereign state. Australia will continue to be a sub-imperial power as long as it remains dependent on another country for its security. Australia should be willing to navigate its own course. It does not matter if Australia is never a great power, but it does matter if it never experiences true sovereignty. To encourage dependency is not the purpose of the alliance, but that has been its outcome. Even without Trump, a re-examination and redefinition of what Australia and the United States want from the alliance is needed.

Conclusion

Involved staff at the Department of Defence must have had a frantic time as they raced to reprioritise the *IIP* and produce the *NDS*. The rush explains some of the incoherency and poor judgement in these documents. The larger share of the responsibility, however, lies with the government, and not because the nation's political leaders demanded complex papers to be written with haste. Rather, it was the messaging that was at fault. Claims of imminent crisis juxtaposed with decades-long acquisition programs do not send a serious message, nor does an inability to provide clearly articulated and soundly thought-through reasons for the decisions taken. The absolute necessity to maintain the unsound investment of a sovereign warship industry, when more relevant and useful sovereign capabilities go begging, defies explanation other than political expediency. For every capability sought and security claim made, the government must be able to answer the question 'Why?' That it does not do so explains the difficulty these documents have in standing up to scrutiny.

The vision for the future ADF remains blurred, too, because of the lack of a clear articulation of a destination. The government has not been able to state a grand strategy, which means that virtually any acquisition can be justified. The greatest problem with these documents, however, is that they have merely shifted the deckchairs rather than changed the course of the nation's future defence policy. They have not embraced disruptive thinking, but have fallen back on the tired but comfortable. The government's claim that it has embarked on a fundamental review of defence policy falls hollow when its recommendations are so predictable and consistent with the past. Existing capabilities are simply replaced by new versions of themselves, while genuine innovation and new ideas fail to gain traction. The potential to embrace the stronger aspect of war – the defence – and take up Australia's natural position as a Strategic Defensive state is missed in the desire to remain a sub-imperial power at all costs. The resulting ADF is one that is again designed to be a micro-sized US military that will be unable to fight on its own without its great partner's assistance: *plus ça change, plus c'est la même chose.*

CONCLUSION: BECOMING A FULLY SOVEREIGN NATION

WITH MUCH FANFARE AND conviction, the Australian government has over the past three years made a series of announcements that claim to represent a fundamental change in the basis of the nation's defence policy, while placing hundreds of billions of dollars on the taxpayer's credit card. As this book has explained, neither AUKUS nor the 2024 *National Defence Strategy* are particularly new in substance, nor especially relevant to the future wars Australia may have to fight. They are best described, along with the 2023 *Defence Strategic Review* and the 2024 *Integrated Investment Program*, as updates to past practice. The government's lack of imagination and reluctance to embrace anything different has resulted in a defence policy that is ill-conceived, badly thought-out and contradictory, and which mandates investment in capabilities that will be of little utility or survivability in the wars Australia will likely have to fight. In addition, the nation's political leaders have embarked upon this policy with minimal explanation of its rationale. In short, Australia's defence policy is broken.

Change is admittedly hard. Like all large organisations the military have institutional cultures that resist transformation as vested interests push back against ideas that threaten the existing hierarchy. All military organisations have sacred cows and die-hard guardians who fight to the bitter end for the way of fighting that they know. The force's senior leaders must show the way, but often they are the ones with the longest experience of the existing practice. I know that it will be hard for the RAN to accept that it can no longer operate surface and subsurface warships, for the RAAF to give primacy to the transport missile launcher, and for the Army to recognise that it should once again become a reserve-dominant force. But the military must embrace hard decisions and accept change if it is to meet the nation's future defence needs.

For the government, change is hard too, but for different reasons. They are responsible for the public purse and are obligated to voters to make the best investment decisions. Mistakes provide fodder for the opposition at the next election, but risk must be taken when warranted and politicians need to lead the nation to a better future. It is with them that responsibility for the development of a grand strategy resides, as does aligning all government departments in the delivery of that strategy's goals.

A government has only one essential function: providing for the defence of the nation it represents and its citizens. The character of war constantly changes, and, therefore, so must the approach to national security. After over 120 years of a defence policy immovably centred on dependency, the geopolitical situation demands something new. The confusion emanating from the United States, and Washington's embrace of autocratic regimes, suggests that a rethink of Australia's policy of dependency would be timely and wise. Politicians must leave their comfort zone and embrace new thinking on how to secure the nation for which they are responsible. Moreover, they must be more honest in the decisions they make, offering clarity rather than obfuscation to the public. They owe the citizenry no less. By adopting the philosophy of the Strategic Defensive, and transforming the ADF, Australia will have a defence policy that is more suited for its security situation than its present one, while also bringing to an end the nation's subservience to a foreign power.

Fortunately, the degree of change required by Australia to be secure into the future is less than it may seem. Certainly Australia must turn its back on the tradition of dependency which to now has served the nation well, but, in light of technological progress, the shifting balance of power in the Western Pacific, the unpredictability of the Trump presidency and the worsening danger of climate change, a new approach is needed. While the Strategic Defensive may seem like a radical idea, that is not the case. It is a longstanding aspect of war, with a history of use by various nations over thousands of years. Strategic Defensive states have certain attributes – they are status quo powers with no designs on anyone. They are also weak states, or at least weaker than those that might do them harm. Status quo, sated and weak are all accurate descriptors of Australia.

To become a Strategic Defensive state will require Australia to again revisit the *Integrated Investment Plan,* but as the recent cancellation of an approved satellite purchase shows, rethinking the *IIP* is entirely feasible. The goal should be to build an ADF whose capability is designed for the defence of the nation rather than to create a boutique military optimised as a subset of the US military. The art of war has entered an era where the defence is in the ascendency and Australia is pursuing the wrong side of the balance. We are now following policies that will lead to strategic defeat.

I am realistic as to the Australian government and the ADF heeding my words. I have long experience in Defence bureaucracy and know that opposition to change is robust. But I also know that change is possible when a leadership embraces new ideas and accepts that other options exist – even though adopting the

Strategic Defensive will require the status quo to be overcome. What Australia wants to avoid is the situation where the driving force behind change is the need to recover from a major defeat, such as the leaders of Prussia had to do following Napoleon's crushing of their army in 1806. Shocked into action, Prussia made fundamental changes to its military and embraced a different philosophy of war, a new organisational design and doctrine that set up the army – and the nation – for success for the rest of the century. Hopefully, the Australian government and the ADF will prove able to accept the Strategic Defensive as the future organising principle for the nation's military, and in doing so avoid the fate of Prussia and other militaries that refuse the necessity and opportunity for change.

ENDNOTES

INTRODUCTION: BREAKING DEPENDENCY

1 The video can be viewed at https://www.youtube.com/watch?app=desktop&v=O9OSbXjuqUU (accessed 20 July 2024).

2 Margaret Simons, 'No Daylight: Inside Labor's Decision to Back AUKUS', *Australian Foreign Affairs*, 19 (October 2023), pp. 50–1; and Kim Carr, 'The Federal Labor Caucus Did Not Endorse AUKUS', *Pearls and Irritations*, 24 March 2023.

3 For one example, see Hal Brands and Michael Beckley, *Danger Zone: The Coming Conflict with China*, New York: WW Norton, 2022.

4 Jim Garamone, 'Official Talks DOD Policy Role in Chinese Pacing Threat, Integrated Deterrence', *US Department of Defense*, 2 June 2021.

5 See Brendan Taylor, *The Four Flashpoints: How Asia Goes to War*, Carlton: La Trobe University Press, 2018, pp. 137–70.

6 Department of Defence, 'Joint Media Statement: Australia to Pursue Nuclear-powered Submarines through New Trilateral Enhanced Security Partnership', 16 September 2021. The UK issued its own similar statement too.

7 'AUKUS Partnership', anthonyalbanese.com.au (accessed 8 December 2023).

8 Simons, 'No Daylight', p. 51.

9 The White House, 'Joint Leaders Statement on AUKUS', 15 September 2021, whitehouse.gov. On the warning time giving to senior Labor parliamentarians, see Kim Carr, 'Labor Was Presented with a Fait Accompli on Aukus, but Scepticism in the Party is Rightly Rising', *The Guardian*, 22 March 2023.

10 Allan Gyngell, 'AUKUS Plans; India; Red Alerts', *Australia in the World Podcast*, Episode 111, 19 March 2023.

11 Benjamin Herscovitch, 'AUKUS Demands More Transparency', *ANU Reporter*, 18 August 2023.

12 On the existence of the American Empire, see Daniel Immerwahr, *How to Hide an Empire: A History of the Greater United States*, New York: Farrer, Straus & Giroux, 2019.

13 On Australia's role as a junior partner, see Clinton Fernandes, *Subimperial Power: Australia in the International Arena*, Melbourne: Melbourne University Press, 2022. See also, Rebecca Strating and Joanne Wallis, *Girt*

by Sea: Re-Imagining Australia's Security, Melbourne: La Trobe University Press, 2024, p. 216.

14 Fred Brenchley, 'The Howard Defence Doctrine', *The Bulletin*, 28 September 1999, p. 2; and David Fickling, 'Australia seen as "America's Deputy Sheriff"', *The Guardian*, 10 September 2004.

15 Henry Reynolds, *Unnecessary Wars*, Sydney: New South, 2016, pp. 38–41.

16 For examples, see Michelle Grattan, '"Armed Neutrality" – A Foreign Policy for Australia?', *The Australian Quarterly*, 4:4 (December 1968), pp. 44–56; Hugh White, *How to Defend Australia*, Carlton: La Trobe University Press, 2019; and Albert Palazzo, *Planning to Not Lose: The Australian Army's New Philosophy of War*, Canberra: Commonwealth of Australia, 2021.

17 'Strategical Report, 1914: Naval Defence of Australia', National Archives of Australia, Melbourne, B6121/186AK.

18 David Martin, *Armed Neutrality for Australia*, Blackburn: Drummond Communications, 1984.

19 Department of Defence, *National Defence: Defence Strategic Review*, Canberra: Commonwealth of Australia, 2023, p. 23.

20 See Albert Palazzo, *Climate Change and National Security: Implications for the Military*, Ft Leavenworth: Army University Press, 2022.

1 UNDERSTANDING AUKUS

1 Andrew Fowler, *Nuked: The Submarine Fiasco that Sank Australia's Sovereignty*, Melbourne: Melbourne University Press, 2024.

2 The fact sheet can be found at: https://pmtranscripts.pmc.gov.au/sites/default/files/AUKUS-factsheet.pdf (accessed 5 December 2023).

3 See Clinton Fernandes, *Island off the Coast of Asia: Instruments of Statecraft in Australian Foreign Policy*, Melbourne: Monash University Press, 2018; and Allan Gyngell and Michael Wesley, *Making Australian Foreign Policy*, 2nd ed, Melbourne: Cambridge University Press, 2007, pp. 233–49.

4 Colonial Defence Committee, *Memorandum on the Defence Forces and Defences of Australia, 1901* (1901), p. 3, National Archives of Australia, A5954, item 1211/2.

5 Ibid.

6 'Defence Scheme for the Commonwealth of Australia' (1905) Australian War Memorial, AWM113, MH1/3, pp. 1–3.

7 'The Federal Premier at Melbourne', *The Sydney Morning Herald*, 15 February 1901, p. 5.

8 Ibid.

9 Joan Beaumont, '"Unitedly We Have Fought": Imperial Loyalty and the Australian War Effort', *International Affairs*, 90:2 (March 2014), p. 411.

10 KS Inglis, *Sacred Places: War Memorials in the Australian Landscape*, Melbourne: Melbourne University Press, 1998, p. 191.
11 Jeffrey Grey, *The Australian Army*, Melbourne: Oxford University Press, 2001, p. 81.
12 Circular Cablegram Z127, 19 June 1940, Lord Caldecote, U.K. Secretary of State for Dominion Affairs, to Sir Geoffrey Whiskard, U.K. High Commissioner in Australia, *Documents on Australian Foreign Policy*, Volume 3.
13 John Curtin, 'The Task Ahead', *The Herald* (Melbourne), 27 December 1941, p. 10.
14 Glen St J Barclay, *Friends in High Places: Australian–American Diplomatic Relations since 1945*, Melbourne: Oxford University Press, 1985, pp. 3–11.
15 Louis Morton, *The Fall of the Philippines*, Washington DC: Office of the Chief of Military History, 1954, pp. 61–8; Mark S Watson, *Chief of Staff: Prewar Plans and Preparations*, Washington DC: Historical Division, 1950, pp. 419–21 and 434–44; and Douglas Gillison, *Royal Australian Air Force, 1939–1942*, Canberra: Australian War Memorial, 1962, pp, 182–4. See also Albert Palazzo, 'Projecting Power: The Development of Queensland as a Base for War', *Journal of the Royal Historical Society of Queensland*, 19:6 (May 2006), pp. 878–91.
16 Jacob Greber, 'Australian Air Bases Assisted with US Strike on Houthi Weapon Stores', *ABC News*, 18 October 2024.
17 Renju Jose and Lewis Jackson, 'US Plans to Deploy B-52s to Northern Australia amid China Tensions – Source', *Reuters*, 1 November 2022.
18 Barclay, *Friends in High Places*, p. 12.
19 Ibid., p. 35.
20 Fernandes, *Island off the Coast of Asia*, p. 38.
21 TB Millar, *Australia in Peace and War: External Relations, 1788–1977*, Canberra: Australian National University Press, 1978, pp. 206–7.
22 *2016 Defence White Paper*, pp. 71 and 121.
23 Ibid., p. 121.
24 Department of Defence, *The Defence of Australia*, Canberra: Commonwealth of Australia, 1987, p. 3.
25 Ibid., pp. 4–5.
26 *DSR*, p. 45.
27 Richard Marles, 'Address: Center for Strategic & International Studies (CSIS)', 12 July 2022.
28 Antony Albanese, 'International Relations: Australia and the United States of America', *Hansard*, House of Representatives, 19 October 2023.
29 *DSR*, p. 25.
30 See Fernandes, *Subimperial Power*.
31 Peter Cochrane, *Best We Forget: The War for White Australia, 1914–18*, Melbourne: Text Publishing, 2018, pp. 47–64 and 201–10.

32 *DSR*, pp. 6 and 23.

33 Allan Gyngell, *Fear of Abandonment: Australia in the World since 1942*, Carlton: La Trobe University Press, 2021, p. 357.

34 David Horner, *The War Game: Australian War Leadership from Gallipoli to Iraq*, Sydney: Allen & Unwin, 2022, p. 185.

35 Australia's Military Commitment to Vietnam, 13 May 1975.

36 On this fear, see Gyngell, *Fear of Abandonment*.

37 Center for Strategic & International Studies, 'A Conversation with Dr. Kurt Campbell and Admiral Michael Gilday on the Strategic and Military Implications of AUKUS', 26 July 2023.

38 Ibid.

39 Hugh White, 'Fatal Shores: AUKUS is a Huge Mistake', in *Australian Foreign Affairs*, 20 (February 2024), p. 42.

40 Australian Submarine Agency, 'AUKUS Agreement for Cooperation on Naval Nuclear Propulsion', 12 August 2024.

41 'Iraq: Authority for Australian Defence Force Military Action', 18 March 2003, National Archives of Australia, A14371, JH03/0124/P1.

42 Jim Acosta, Kylie Atwood and Maegan Vazquez, 'France Recalls its Ambassadors to the US and Australia over New National Security Partnership', *CNN*, 18 September 2021.

43 'Australia Announces Compensation Deal with France for Scrapped Submarine Contract', *France 24*, 11 June 2022.

44 Ministry of Foreign Affairs of the Republic of Indonesia, 'Statement on Australia's Nuclear Powered Submarine Program', 17 September 2021.

45 Stephen Dziedzic, 'Beijing Warns AUKUS Submarine Project Sets a "Dangerous Precedent" and Threatens Non-Proliferation', *ABC News*, 12 July 2022; and Ron Huisken, 'What China's Condemnation of AUKUS Says about Beijing', *The Strategist*, 28 July 2022.

46 *Navy Virginia-Class Submarine Program and AUKUS Submarine Proposal: Background and Issues for Congress*, Washington, DC: Congressional Research Service, 2023, pp. 14–16.

47 John Christianson, Sean Monaghan and Di Cooke, *AUKUS Pillar Two: Advancing the Capabilities of the United States, United Kingdom, and Australia*, Washington, DC: CSIS, 2023.

48 Amy Remeikis, 'Australia to Buy Tomahawk Cruise Missiles in $1.7bn Spend on Long-range Defence Capability', *The Guardian*, 21 August 2023.

49 Department of Defence, 'AUKUS Defense Ministers Meeting Joint Statement', 2 December 2023; and Defence Media Release, 'First Royal Australian Navy Officers Assigned to US Virginia Class Submarines', 18 April 2024.

50 'AUKUS Defense Ministers Meeting Joint Statement', 2 December 2023.

51 Rick Moore, 'Submarine Tendered Maintenance Period Complete, USS *Hawaii* (SSN776) Departs HMAS *Stirling*', *US Navy*, 10 September 2024.

52 The White House, 'Joint Leaders Statement on AUKUS', 13 March 2013.
53 Prime Minister of Australia, 'Joint Leaders' Statement to Mark the Second Anniversary of AUKUS', 15 September 2023.
54 'AUKUS Agreement for Cooperation on Naval Nuclear Propulsion'.
55 Peter Edwards, *Permanent Friends? Historical Reflections of the Australian–American Alliance*, Sydney: Lowy Institute, 2005, p. 2.
56 Coral Bell, *Dependent Ally: A Study in Australian Foreign Policy*, Melbourne: Oxford University Press, 1988, p. 2.
57 Daniel Hurst and Julian Borger, 'Aukus: Nuclear Submarines Deal Will Cost Australia up to $368bn,' *The Guardian*, 14 March 2023.
58 Defence Media Release, 'Passage of Priority AUKUS Submarine and Export Control Exemption Legislation by the United States Congress', 15 December 2023.
59 House of Representatives, 'National Defense Authorization Act for Fiscal Year 2024: Conference Report to Accompany HR 2670', December 2023, pp. 379–84.
60 'AUKUS Agreement for Cooperation on Naval Nuclear Propulsion'.
61 *DSR*, p. 61.
62 *Navy Virginia-Class Submarine Program and AUKUS Submarine Proposal*, pp. 23–52.

2 AUSTRALIA'S THREAT ENVIRONMENT

1 See Allan Behm, *The Odd Couple, The Australia–America Relationship*, Perth: Upswell, 2024.
2 For examples, see Elizabeth Kolbert, *Field Notes from a Catastrophe: A Frontline Report on Climate* Change, London: Bloomsbury, 2007; Bill McGuire, *Hot House Earth: An Inhabitant's Guide*, London: Icon Books, 2022; Todd Miller, *Storming the Wall: Climate Change, Migration and Homeland Security*, San Francisco: City Lights, 2017; and David Spratt and Philip Sutton, *Climate Code Red: The Case for Emergency Action*, Carlton: Scribe Publications, 2009.
3 The White House, 2022 *National Security Strategy*, whitehouse.gov, 12 October 2022, p. 23. How China will accomplish this is explained in Rush Doshi, *The Long Game: China's Grand Strategy to Displace American Order*, Oxford: Oxford University Press, 2021.
4 The White House, *2022 Indo-Pacific Strategy of the United States*, whitehouse.gov, February 2022.
5 'Full text of Xi Jinping's Report at 19th CPC National Congress', *China Daily*, 4 November 2017.
6 Timothy R Heath, Derek Grossman and Asha Clark, *China's Quest for Global Primacy: An Analysis of Chinese International and Defense Strategies to Outcompete the United States*, Santa Monica: Rand Corporation, 2021, p. 43.

7 'President Xi Expounds Best Approach to Reunification', *China Plus*, 2 January 2019.
8 Heath, Grossman and Clark, *China's Quest for Global Primacy*, pp. 42–3.
9 Jonathan P Wong, and others, *New Directions for Projecting Land Power in the Indo-Pacific*, Santa Monica: Rand Corporation, 2022, pp. 14–15.
10 Elbridge A Colby, *A Strategy of Denial: American Defense in an Age of Great Power Conflict*, New Haven: Yale University Press, 2022, p. 5.
11 Ibid., p. 9.
12 2022 *National Security Strategy*, p. 24.
13 Colby, *A Strategy of Denial*, p. 21.
14 Department of Defence, *2020 Defence Strategic Update*, Canberra: Commonwealth of Australia, 2020, p. 11.
15 *DSR*, p. 27.
16 Ibid., p. 23.
17 Richard Marles, Speech, 'News Corp's Defending Australia: Australian War Memorial', 22 May 2023.
18 Department of Prime Minister and Cabinet, 'Transcript of the Prime Minister the Hon John Howard MP interview with Tracey Grimshaw, the Today Show', 21 November 2002.
19 Penny Wong, 'ASEAN-Australian Special Summit 2024 – Keynote Address to the Maritime Cooperation Forum, Speech', 4 March 2024.
20 Hugh White, *The China Choice: Why America Should Share Power*, Melbourne: Black Inc, 2013.
21 Daniel Hurst, 'Australia Cannot be "Passive Bystanders" in a War Between US and China, Richard Marles Says', *The Guardian*, 18 October 2023.
22 See, for example, Graham Allison, *Destined for War: Can America and China Escape Thucydides's Trap?*, Boston: Houghton Mifflin Harcourt, 2017; and Brands and Beckley, *Danger Zone*.
23 For greenhouse gas measurements, see 'Recent Daily Average Mauna Loa CO_2' (accessed 17 December 2024). See also 'Trends in Atmospheric Carbon Dioxide', *NOAA Global Monitoring Laboratory* (accessed 24 January 2024).
24 Rebecca Lindsey and Luann Dahlman, 'Climate Change: Global Temperature', *NOAA*, 18 January 2024.
25 Michael T Klare, *All Hell Breaking Loose: The Pentagon's Perspective on Climate Change*, New York: Metropolitan Books, 2019, p. 17; and Spencer Ackerman, 'Climate Change is the Biggest Threat in the Pacific, Says Top U.S. Admiral', *Wired*, 11 March 2013.
26 The White House, *Indo-Pacific Strategy of the United States*, 2022, whitehouse.gov.
27 'Chronology of U.S. Military Statements and Actions on Climate Change and Security', *The Center for Climate & Security*, 16 February 2019.

28 David Vergun, 'Defence Secretary Calls Climate Crisis an Existential Threat', *DOD News*, 22 April 2021.
29 'Secretary-General's Remarks at Opening of the World Climate Action Summit', *United Nations*, 2 December 2024.
30 Patrick Greenfield, '"Essential to Act Now" to Prevent Chaotic Climate Breakdown, Warns UN Chief', *The Guardian*, 8 November 2024.
31 'The Paris Agreement', United Nations, un.org (accessed 23 January 2024).
32 'Copernicus: 2023 is the Hottest Year on Record, with Global Temperatures Close to the 1.5°C Limit', *Copernicus Climate Change Service*, 9 January 2024.
33 'Betrayal in Baku: Developed Countries Fail People and Planet', *Climate Action Network*, 23 November 2024.
34 Richard Marles, 'Address: Center for Strategic & International Studies (CSIS)', 12 July 2022.
35 Garry Cook and others, 'Australia's Black Summer of Fire Was Not Normal – and We Can Prove it', *CSIRO*, 29 November 2021.
36 Department of Foreign Affairs and Trade, 'Australia–Tuvalu Falepili Union Treaty', September 2024.
37 CNA Military Advisory Board, *National Security and the Accelerating Risks of Climate Change*, Alexandria: CNA Corporation, 2014, p. 2.
38 National Intelligence Council, 'Implications for US National Security of Anticipated Climate Change', 2016.
39 Office of the Director of National Intelligence, 'Worldwide Threat Assessment of the US Intelligence Community', Senate Select Committee on Intelligence (2013), p. 9.
40 John Mecklin, ed., 'A Moment of Historic Danger: It is Still 90 Seconds to Midnight', *Bulletin of the Atomic Scientists*, 23 January 2024.
41 *DSR*, pp. 41–2.
42 Defence Media Release, 'Navy's Enhanced Lethality Surface Combatant Fleet', 20 February 2024.
43 See Thomas Hobbes, *Leviathan*, Ware: Wordsworth Editions, 2014.
44 Mark Ogge, Audrey Quicke and Rod Campbell, *Undermining Climate Action: The Australian Way*, Canberra: The Australia Institute, 2021, p. 20.
45 Behm, *The Odd Couple*.
46 Alexander Palmer and others, 'Unpacking China's Naval Buildup', *CSIS*, 5 June 2024.
47 'The Complex Challenges Facing China's Economic Future', *World Finance* (accessed 28 January 2024); Rebecca Feng, 'China's Colossal Hidden-debt Problem is Coming to a Head', *The Wall Street Journal*, 5 December 2023; '5 Pressing Environmental Issues China is Dealing with in 2024', *Earth.Org*, 17 January 2024; Frank Lavin, 'China's Population Problem Worsens',

Forbes, 5 December 2023; and Rob Brooks, 'China's Biggest Problem? Too Many Men', *UNSW Newsroom*, 15 November 2012.

48 Ivo Daalder, 'What Another Trump Presidency Would Mean for NATO', *Politico*, 25 January 2024.

49 Max Boot, 'If Trump Wins, He Will Destroy the American-led World Order', *The Washington Post*, 31 January 2024.

50 John Hewson, 'What Donald Trump's Re-election Would Mean for Australia', *The Saturday Paper*, 27 January 2024.

51 Horner, *The War Game*, p. 156.

52 Ibid., p. 159.

53 Rod McGuirk, 'Australia to Send Military Personnel to Help Protect Red Sea Shipping but no Warship', *Associated Press*, 21 December 2023; and Department of Defence Media Release, 'Increased Support for Strike Action against Houthi', 29 February 2024.

54 Andrew Bacevich, *America's War for the Greater Middle East*, New York: Random House, 2017, p. 143.

55 Sarah E Mendelson, 'The US is Leaving Millions Behind: American Exceptionalism Needs to Change by 2030', *Brookings*, 10 April 2023; and Jean M Twenge, 'The Death of American Exceptionalism', *The Atlantic*, 25 October 2024.

56 Andrew Bacevich, *Washington Rules: America's Path to Permanent War*, New York: Henry Holt, 2010, p. 162.

57 Karen Middleton, *An Unwinnable War: Australia in Afghanistan*, Carlton: Melbourne University Publishing, 2011, p. 309.

58 Ibid., p. 315.

59 Thucydides, *The Landmark Thucydides*, Robert B Strassler, ed., New York: Free Press, 1996, p. 43.

3 DESIGNING AUSTRALIA'S FUTURE DEFENCE POLICY

1 BH Liddell Hart, *Thoughts on War*, Staplehurst: Spellmount, 1999, p. 115.

2 Donald Horne, *The Lucky Country, Australia in the Sixties*, Sydney: Angus & Robertson, 1964, p. 217.

3 Allan Behm, 'Australia's Perceptions of Strategic Risks and Policy Reponses', Presentation at the APLN–ELN Canberra Roundtable, 7 December 2022.

4 Penny Wong, 'National Press Club Address, Australian Interests in a Regional Balance of Power', 17 April 2023.

5 Michael Heath, 'China Isn't "Status-quo Power", Aussie PM Albanese Tells US State Department', *Bloomberg*, 27 October 2023.

6 'Trading Economics: Australia GDP', tradingeconomics.com/australia/gdp; and 'Trading Economics: China GDP', tradingeconomics.com/china/gdp (both accessed 15 August 2024).

7 Einar H Dyvik, 'Gross Domestic Product of G20 Countries in 2022, with Projection for 2027', *Statista*, 17 October 2023. See also White, *How to Defend Australia*, pp. 38–42.

8 On the management of the Vietnam War supply chain, see Albert Palazzo, *Australian Military Operations in Vietnam*, Canberra: Commonwealth of Australia, 2009, pp. 166–9.

9 Marles, 'Address: Center for Strategic & International Studies'.

10 Robert A Pape, *Bombing to Win: Air Power and Coercion in War*, Ithaca: Cornell University Press, 1996, p. 314.

11 Vegetius, *Epitome of Military Science*, NP Millar, trans., Liverpool: Liverpool University Press, 2011, p. 63.

12 'Finland Among the Best in the World', *Statistics Finland*, www.stat.fi (accessed 21 February 2024); and Leo Laikola, 'Finland Crowned World's Happiest for Sixth Year Running in Ranking Dominated by Nordics', *Bloomberg*, 20 March 2023.

13 Colmar Freiherr von der Goltz, *The Conduct of War*, GF Leverson, trans., London: Keegan Paul, Trench, Trübner & Co. Ltd., 1908, p. 8.

14 Liddell Hart, *Thoughts on War*, p. 20.

15 Carl von Clausewitz, *On War*, Michael Howard and Peter Paret, eds & trans, Princeton: Princeton University Press, 1989, p. 128.

16 Ibid.

17 David Jordan and others, *Understanding Modern Warfare*, Cambridge: Cambridge University Press, 2008, p. 10.

18 Andreas Herberg-Rothe, *Clausewitz's Puzzle: The Political Theory of War*, Oxford: Oxford University Press, 2007, p. 112.

19 Clausewitz, *On War*, pp. 357–9.

20 Albert Palazzo, 'Crossing 2000 Kilometres of Death', *Land Power Forum*, 17 September 2019.

21 Christopher A Lawrence, *War by the Numbers: Understanding Conventional Combat*, Lincoln: Potomac Books, 2017, pp. 14–15, 329–38.

22 Clausewitz, *On War*, pp. 379–80.

23 Ibid., p. 370.

24 Goltz, *The Conduct of War*, pp. 22–32.

25 Julian S Corbett, *Principles of Maritime Strategy*, Mineola: Dover, 2004, p. 69.

26 Toshi Yoshihara and James R Holmes, *Red Star over the Pacific: China's Rise and the Challenge to US Maritime Strategy*, 2nd ed., Annapolis: Naval Institute Press, 2018, pp. 175–9.

27 Peter Turchin, 'America is Headed Towards Collapse', *The Atlantic*, 2 June 2023; and Ross Douthat, 'The American Empire in Retreat,' *The New York Times*, 4 September 2021.

28 Bruce Stokes, 'Could the United States be Headed for a National Divorce?', *Chatham House*, 20 February 2024; and 'Politics and Elections, Economist/ YouGov Poll: August 20–23, 2022', 24 August 2022, today.yougov.com. See also Stephen Marche, *The Next Civil War: Dispatches from the American Future*, New York: Simon & Schuster, 2023.
29 Charles Bethea, 'The Americans Prepping for a Second Civil War', *The New Yorker*, 4 November 2024.

4 LAYING THE FOUNDATION FOR THE STRATEGIC DEFENSIVE

1 David Watt and Nic Brangwin, 'Defence', Parliament of Australia, 2 May 2023.
2 Marcus Hellyer, 'Defence Budget 2023–24: Living in the Past', *Strategic Analysis Australia*; and Department of the Treasury, *Budget 2023–24: Stronger Foundations for a Better Future*, Canberra: Commonwealth of Australia, 2023, p. 67.
3 Andrew Shearer, 'Australian Defence in the Era of Austerity: Mind the Expectation Gap', in Gary J Schmitt, ed., *A Hard Look at Hard Power: Assessing the Defense Capabilities of Key US Allies and Security Partners*, Carlisle Barracks: Strategic Studies Institute, 2015, pp. 38–9.
4 Max Blenkin, '2023–24 Defence Budget at First Glance', *Australian Defence Magazine*, 9 May 2023.
5 Watt and Brangwin, 'Defence'.
6 Daniel Hurst, 'Australia Moves to Prop Up Aukus with $4.6bn Pledge to Help Clear Rolls-Royce Nuclear Reactor Bottlenecks in the UK', *The Guardian*, 21 March 2024.
7 Daniel Hurst, 'Federal Budget Squirrels Away $30bn to Lift Defence Funding Over Decade', *The Guardian*, 9 May 2023.
8 Andrew Tillett, 'Defence Projects Face Axe to Fund New Weapons', *Australian Financial Review*, 27 November 2023. See also *DSR*, pp. 95–6.
9 Department of Defence, 'Press Conference, Parliament House', 24 April 2023.
10 Hellyer, 'Defence Budget 2023–24'.
11 Jennifer Parker and others, *The Big Squeeze: ASPI Defence Budget Brief 2023–2024*, Canberra: Australian Strategic Policy Institute, 2023, p. 5.
12 Marcus Hellyer, 'Unpacking the Numbers in Defence's New Integrated Investment Plan', *Strategic Analysis Australia* (accessed 3 May 2024).
13 Department of Defence, *Integrated Investment Program*, Canberra: Commonwealth of Australia, 2024, p. 9.
14 Hellyer, 'Unpacking the Numbers in Defence's New Integrated Investment Plan'.
15 Gyngell, *Australian in the World*.

16 Gordon Arthur, 'Maritime Capabilities Take Lion's Share of Australia's Future Defence Investment', *Naval News*, 19 April 2024.
17 Tender, 'Land 156 Counter Small-Uncrewed Aerial Systems, Systems Integration Partner', 21 November 2024.
18 John Guilmartin, 'Technology and Strategy: What are the Limits?', in Michael Howard and John Guilmartin, *Two Historians in Technology and War*, Carlisle Barracks: Strategic Studies Institute, 1994, pp. 11–13.
19 On the Roman way of war, see Vegetius, *Epitome of Military Science* and Jonathan P Roth, *Roman Warfare*, Cambridge: Cambridge University Press, 2009.
20 See Mao Tse-Tung, *On Guerrilla Warfare*, Samuel B Griffith, trans, New York: Praeger Publishers, 1961.
21 Department of Defence, *National Defence Strategy*, Canberra: Commonwealth of Australia, 2024, pp. 27–8. On the meaning of impactful projection, see Kuper, 'With NDS and IIP Out of the Way, We're Still no Closer to Understanding What is Meant by "Impactful Projection"', *Defence Connect*, 30 April 2024.
22 Australian Security Leaders Climate Group, *Too Hot to Handle: The Scorching Reality of Australia's Climate-Security Failure*, Canberra: ASLCG, 2024, p. 9.
23 *NDS*, p. 46.
24 Bacevich, *America's War for the Greater Middle East*, p. 143.
25 Ibid., p. 110.
26 Sun Tzu, *The Art of War*, Samuel B Griffith, trans., Oxford: Oxford University Press, 1963, p. 77.
27 Gregory R Copley, 'AUKUS Moves Toward Success, Except in Delivering SSNs and a Strategic Capability to Australia', *Defence & Foreign Affairs*, 42:7 (6 March 2024), p. 2.
28 Richard Rosecrance and Arthur A Stein, 'Beyond Realism: The Study of Grand Strategy', in Rosecrance and Stein, eds, *The Domestic Bases of Grand Strategy*, Ithaca: Cornell University Press, 1993, p. 4.
29 Colin S Gray, *Fighting Talk: Forty Maxims on War, Peace and Strategy*, Dulles: Potomac Books, 2009, pp. 82–5.
30 Edward Mead Earle, 'Introduction', in Edward Mead Earle, ed., *Makers of Modern Strategy: Military Thought from Machiavelli to Hitler*, Princeton: Princeton University Press, 1971, p. viii.
31 David Jordan and others, *Understanding Modern Warfare*, p. 10.
32 Williamson Murray, 'Thoughts on Grand Strategy', in Williamson Murray, Richard Hart Sinnreich and James Lacy, eds, *The Shaping of Grand Strategy: Policy, Diplomacy, and War*, Cambridge: Cambridge University Press, 2011, p. 11.
33 Ibid., p. 9.

34 Ibid., p. 5.
35 'Refined Petroleum in Australia, 2022', *The Observatory of Economic Complexity* (accessed 16 March 2024). On transit security, see Richard Oloruntoba and others, 'Conflict in the South China Sea Threatens 90% of Australia's Fuel Imports: Study', *The Conversation*, 21 August 2022.
36 Saul Griffith, *The Big Switch: Australia's Electric Future*, Collingwood: Black Inc, 2022.
37 Liam Carter, Audrey Quicke and Alia Armistead, *Over a Barrel: Addressing Australia's Liquid Fuel Security*, Canberra: The Australia Institute, 2022, p. 16.
38 Department of Climate Change, Energy, the Environment and Water, 'Australia's Fuel Security'.
39 Alan Dupont, *Grand Strategy, National Security and the Australian Defence Force*, Sydney: Lowy Institute for International Policy, 2005, p. 1.
40 Copley, 'AUKUS Moves Toward Success', p. 2.
41 On Lincoln, see Elliot A Cohen, *Supreme Command: Soldiers, Statesmen, and Leadership in Wartime*, New York: The Free Press, 2002, pp. 30–33. See also Williamson Murray, 'The American Civil War', in John Andreas Olsen and Colin S Gray, eds, *The Practice of Strategy: From Alexander the Great to the Present*, Oxford: Oxford University Press, 2011, pp. 199–218.
42 Peter R Mansoor, 'US Grand Strategy in the Second World War', in Williamson Murray and Richard Hart Sinnreich, eds, *Successful Strategies: Triumphing in War and Peace from Antiquity to the Present*, Cambridge: Cambridge University Press, 2014, pp. 314–52.
43 John Lewis Gaddis, 'Grand Strategy in the Second Term', *Foreign Affairs* (January/February 2005); Hal Brands, *American Grand Strategy in the Age of Trump*, Washington, DC: Brookings Institution Press, 2018 p. 169.
44 Colin S Gray, 'Why Strategy is Difficult', in Colin S Gray, *Strategy and History: Essays on Theory and Practice*, Milton Park: Routledge, 2006, pp. 74–80.
45 Copley, 'AUKUS Moves Toward Success', p. 6.

5 WHAT NEEDS TO BE DONE

1 *NDS*, p. 25.
2 *DSR*, p. 6.
3 Ibid., p. 23.
4 *NDS*, p. 11.
5 Department of Defence, *2016 Defence White Paper*, Canberra: Commonwealth of Australia, 2016, pp. 30, 33 and 41.
6 Albert Palazzo, *The Future of War Debate in Australia: Why Has There Not Been One? Has the Need for One Now Arrived?*, Canberra: Land Warfare Studies Centre, 2012, pp. 21–2.

7 *NDS*, pp. 28–9.
8 *DSR*, p. 45; and *NDS*, p. 46.
9 Department of Defence, *Naval Shipbuilding and Sustainment Plan: Evolving the Enterprise*, Canberra: Commonwealth of Australia, 2024.
10 John Stone, 'Conventional Deterrence and the Challenge of Credibility', *Contemporary Security Policy*, 33:1 (2012) p. 109; and Steve Chan, 'Extended Deterrence in the Taiwan Strait: Discerning Resolve and Commitment', *American Association of Chinese Studies*, 21 (June 2014), p. 84.
11 'Washington Quotes on Military', mountvernon.org (accessed 6 May 2024).
12 Andrew Tillet, 'Slim Pickings for Navy as it Struggles to Recruit', *Australian Financial Review*, 5 January 2024.
13 Kym Bergmann, 'Navy Surface Fleet Facing a Worrying Fall in Numbers Later this Decade', *Asia Pacific Defence Reporter*, 50:2 (March 2024), pp. 12–13.
14 Department of Defence, *Defending Australia in the Asia Pacific Century: Force 2030*, Canberra: Commonwealth of Australia, 2009, p. 70.
15 Watt and Brangwin, 'Defence'; and Tory Shepard, 'Mind the Capability Gap: What Happens if Collins Class Submarines Retire Before Nuclear Boats are Ready', *The Guardian*, 28 February 2023.
16 Department of Defence, *Enhanced Lethality Surface Combatant Fleet*, Canberra: Commonwealth of Australia, 2024.
17 Andrew Greene, 'Defence Admits "Poorly Executed" Process in $45 Billion Future Frigate Selection', *ABC News*, 13 November 2023.
18 Rowan Moffitt, 'Australia's Hunter Frigate Project Should be Sunk', *Australian Financial Review*, 20 December 2023.
19 David Shackleton, 'The Future of the RAN's Surface Combatant Fleet', *The Strategist*, 14 August 2023.
20 David Shackleton, *The Hunter Frigate: An Assessment*, Canberra: Australian Strategic Policy Institute, 2022, p. 38.
21 David Shackleton, 'Australia's Hunter-class Frigate Program Must be Stopped and Redirected', *The Strategist*, 28 April 2022.
22 *Enhanced Lethality Surface Combatant Fleet*, p. 16.
23 David H Driesbach, 'The Arsenal Ship and the U.S. Navy: A Revolution in Military Affairs Perspective', MA Thesis, Monterey: US Navy, Naval Postgraduate School, 1996, p. 23–6.
24 Eunhyuk Cha, 'South Korea's DSME to Design Arsenal Ship for ROK Navy', *Naval News*, 14 April 2023.
25 Department of Defence, 'Press Conference, Henderson, Western Australia', 22 February 2024.
26 Defence Media Release, 'Securing Continuous Naval Shipbuilding at Henderson Shipyard in Western Australia', 23 November 2023; and Defence Media Release, 'Press Conference, Henderson, Western Australia', 22 February 2024.

27 Matthew Doran, 'Australia's Surface Navy Fleet is Being Reshaped. Here's How it Will Change', *ABC News*, 20 February 2024.
28 Defence Media Release, 'General Purpose Frigate Milestone Reached with Down-selection of Shipbuilders', 25 November 2024.
29 Defence Media Release, 'Offshore Patrol Vessels', n.d., defence.gov.au.
30 Brendan Nicholson, 'Navy Chief Mark Hammond: With a Well-designed Campaign, Surface Warships Can Operate in a High Intensity Conflict', *The Strategist*, 22 February 2024.
31 *Enhanced Lethality Surface Combatant Fleet*, p. 10; Bergmann, 'Navy Surface Fleet Facing a Worrying Fall in Numbers Later this Decade', pp. 14–15; and Department of Defence, *Integrated Investment Program*, p. 36.
32 *Enhanced Lethality Surface Combatant Fleet*, p. 10, and 'Maritime Border Command', *Australian Border Force*, abf.gov.au.
33 Copley, 'AUKUS Moves Toward Success', p. 3.
34 *Navy Virginia-Class Submarine Program and AUKUS Submarine (Pillar 1) Project: Background and Issues for Congress*, Washington, DC: Congressional Research Service, 2024, pp. 21–37. For the letter, see https://courtney.house.gov/sites/evo-subsites/courtney.house.gov/files/evo-media-document/FY25%20Submarine%20Support%20Letter_Web.pdf (accessed 9 January 2025).
35 Kym Bergmann, 'US Virginia Submarine Production Shortfall Worsens', *APDR*, 12 March 2024.
36 Peter Briggs, 'The Sad State of the Royal Navy Submarine Capability – and the Implications for Australia', *The Strategist*, 30 January 2024.
37 Hurst, 'Australia Moves to Prop Up AUKUS with $4.6bn'; and Pamela Tickell, 'Investigation into BAE Nuclear Shipyard Fire', *BBC News*, 31 October 2024.
38 Roger Bradbury and others, *Transparent Oceans? The Coming SSBN Counter-detection Task May be Insuperable*, Canberra: National Security College, 2020; Bryan Clark, *The Emerging Era in Undersea Warfare*, Washington, DC: CSBA, 2015; Rhys Kissell, 'New Study Suggests Climate Change Will Make Submarine Warfare More Complex', *The Strategist*, 20 December 2023; Natasha Bajema, 'Will AI Steal Submarines' Stealth?', *IEEE Spectrum*, 16 July 2022; and Sebastian Brixey-Williams, 'Prospects for Game-changes in Submarine-detection Technology', *The Strategist*, 22 August 2020.
39 Natasha Bajema, 'Rewriting the Rules of Submarine Stealth', *Foreign Policy*, 16 December 2024.
40 Bryan Clark and Timothy A Walton, *Fighting into the Bastions: Getting Noisier to Sustain the US Undersea Advantage*, Washington, DC: Hudson Institute, 2023.

41 Peter Briggs, 'How Many Nuclear-powered Submarines for Australia?', *The Strategist*, 12 October 2023.
42 Defence Media Release, 'Navy's Enhanced Lethality Surface Combatant Fleet', Department of Defence, 20 February 2024.
43 *NDS*, p. 23.
44 Department of Foreign Affairs and Trade, 'Australia's Trade in Goods and Services by Top 15 Partners', 2022.
45 Strating and Wallis, *Girt by Sea*, p. 224.
46 Australian Maritime Authority, 'Year in Review', amsa.gov.au, 2021 (accessed 19 December 2024).
47 Department of Infrastructure, *Strategic Fleet Taskforce*, Canberra: Commonwealth of Australia, 2023.
48 '15 Biggest Shipping Companies in the World', *Marine Digital*, marine-digital.com (accessed 26 March 2024).
49 'Top 10 Largest Shipping Companies with Bulk Carriers', *Marine Digital*, marine-digital.com (accessed 26 March 2024).
50 'Australian Trade Profile', *The Observatory of Economic Complexity*, oec.world/en (accessed 29 March 2024).
51 See Albert Palazzo, 'The End of Maritime Strategy', in Justin Jones, ed., *A Maritime School of Strategic Thought for Australia*, Canberra: Sea Power Centre – Australia, 2013, pp. 113–19.
52 Wayne P Hughes, Jr and Robert Girrier, *Fleet Tactics and Naval Operations*, 3rd ed., Annapolis: Naval Institute Press, 2018, pp. 115, 128 and 132.
53 TX Hammes, 'The Tactical Defense Becomes Dominant Again', *JFQ*, 103 (4th Qtr, 2021), p. 12.
54 Henry J Hendrix, *At What Cost a Carrier*, Washington, DC: Center for a New American Security, 2013, pp. 8–9.
55 David C Gompert, *Sea Power and American Interests in the Western Pacific*, Santa Monica: RAND, 2013, p. 150.
56 Brandon J Weichert, 'The Age of Big Powerhouse US Navy Warships is all Over Now', *The National Interest*, 8 May 2024.
57 David Axe, 'In One Massive Attack, Ukrainian Missiles Hit Four Russian Ships – Including Three Landing Vessels', *Forbes*, 26 March 2024.
58 Wayne P Hughes, 'Naval Maneuver Warfare', *Naval War College Review*, 41:3 (September 1997), pp. 36–7.
59 Stephen Kuper, 'We Know What's in, but What's Out? Assessing the Reprioritisations and the "Cuts" of the IIP and the NDS', *Defence Connect*, 29 April 2024.
60 Data taken from RAAF, 'RAAF Aircraft', airforce.gov.au (accessed 28 March 2024).

61 'Rapid Dragon', Air Force Research Lab, afresearchlab.com (accessed 28 March 2024).
62 US Defence Security Cooperation Agency, 'Australia – C-130J-30 Aircraft', 2 November 2022.
63 *DSR*, pp. 59–60.
64 Mark Mankowski, 'What is Littoral Manoeuvre? – Part 1', *Land Power Forum*, 24 August 2023.
65 Aaron-Matthew Lariosa, 'Australian Army Shifting Priorities to Amphibious, Littoral Operations', *USNI News*, 2 October 2023.
66 'Australia on Track for Missile Manufacturing and Increasing Long Range Strike Capability', *Defence Media*, 16 January 2024.
67 Albert Palazzo, 'Adding Bang to the Boat: A Call to Weaponise Land 8710', *Land Power Forum*, 1 December 2020.
68 *IIP*, p. 59.
69 Tender, 'Land 156 Counter Small-Uncrewed Aerial Systems, Systems Integration Partner'.
70 Isabelle Oderberg, 'Australian Military Buy $5m Laser-based Anti-drone System', *The Guardian*, 26 March 2024.
71 Leo Purdy, 'Understanding Armour and Why the IFV Matters to Australia', *ADM*, 26 July 2022.
72 RAAF, 'Defence Space Strategy', airforce.gov.au (accessed 29 March 2024).
73 Defence Media Release, 'Defence to Prioritise Resilient Satellite Communications Capability', 4 November 2024.
74 *IIP*, pp. 47–51.
75 Malcom Davis, 'Force's Bold Launch Into Space Projects', *ASPI*, 26 February 2019; and Andrew McLaughlin, 'ADF Project JP9102 SATCOM Bids Go in the Box', *Australian Defence Business Review*, 11 January 2022.
76 *DSR*, pp. 54–5.
77 *NDS*, pp. 38–41; and Andrew Greene, '$7 Billion Project to Create Australian Military Satellites Axed Amid Defence Spending Review', *ABC News*, 4 November 2024.
78 Richard Marles, Address to Center for Strategic & International Studies, Department of Defence, 12 July 2022.
79 *IIP*, p. 51.
80 Department of Defence, *2020 Force Structure Plan*, Canberra: Commonwealth of Australia, 2020.
81 Albert Palazzo, 'Hardened Bases Needed for ADF's New Hardware', *The Strategist*, 3 December 2020.
82 *IIP*, pp. 85–7.
83 Department of Defence, *Strategic Review 1993*, Canberra: Commonwealth of Australia, 1993, p. 7.

84 Stephan Frühling and Andrew O'Neil, *Partners in Deterrence: US Nuclear Weapons and Alliances in Europe and Asia*, Manchester: Manchester University Press, 2021, pp. 165 and 184.

85 Honoré M Catudal, *Nuclear Deterrence: Does it Deter?*, London: Mansell Publishing, 1985, pp. 37–9.

86 Henry Kissinger, *American Foreign Policy*, New York: WW Norton & Co., 1974, p. 15.

87 Sewell Chan, 'Stanislav Petrov, Soviet Officer who Helped Avert Nuclear War, Is Dead at 77', *The New York Times*, 18 September 2017.

88 On this and other incidents, see Eric Schlosser, *Command and Control: Nuclear Weapons, the Damascus Accident, and the Illusion of Safety*, New York: Penguin Press, 2013.

89 Alan Robock, 'Nuclear Smoke and the Climatic Effects of Nuclear War', in Helen Caldicott, ed., *Sleepwalking to Armageddon: The Threat of Nuclear Annihilation*, New York: The New Press, 2017, pp. 27–32; Alan Robock, and others, 'How Fear of Nuclear Winter Has Helped Save the World, so Far', *Atmospheric Chemistry and Physics*, 23:12, 19 June 2023, pp. 6691–6701; and Mark Maslin, 'Nuclear War Would be More Devastating for Earth's Climate than Cold War Predictions – Even with Fewer Weapons', *The Conversation*, 2 August 2023.

INDEX

Locators followed by a 't' refer to a table on that page.